ICE BREAKERS 6

67 NO PREP, NO PROP ACTIVITIES!

By Valerie Lippoldt Mack and Matthew Udland

Thank you to our children and spouses for encouraging us to spread joy through games that people can play. Thank you, Stevie, Zane, Lucy and James. Thank you, Tom and Leslie. We appreciate you believing in us every day and for giving us so many reasons to smile.

Thank you, Henry Waters, Joel Knudsen, Nancy Wesche, the Butler Fine Arts Family and everyone else that provided inspiration to the games. Just know you are so appreciated. If you see yourself in any part of this book, know that your lessons continue to make an impact on a bigger audience.

Thank you, Greg Gilpin. You continue to inspire and push – and sometimes shove. The world is a better place because of you and your musical contributions.

Lastly, thank you to all our students and friends who have allowed us our games.

SHAWNEE PRESS

EXCLUSIVELY DISTRIBUTED BY

HAL•LEONARD®

7777 W. BLUEMOUND RD. P.O. BOX 13819 MILWAUKEE, WI 53213
In Australia Contact:
Hal Leonard Australia Pty. Ltd.
4 Lentara Court
Cheltenham, Victoria, 3192 Australia
Email: ausadmin@halleonard.com.au

Visit Shawnee Press Online at **www.shawneepress.com**
Visit Hal Leonard Online at **www.halleonard.com**

Table of Contents

CELEBRATING DIVERSITY
Unifying and Encouraging Individuality

PROBLEM SOLVING
Turning Stressful Conditions into Working Conditions

SUPPORT AND APPRECIATE
2, 4, 6, 8 Who do we appreciate!?

ADDITIONAL TECH SUPPORT
Using Technology for Personal Connections

Foreword

The positive response to *IceBreakers 1* (35010427) and *IceBreakers 2* (35010428) made us realize the need for a new IceBreaker book. Teachers seem to have less time and reduced budgets for planning and creating. *IceBreakers 3* presents simple activities with a purpose. Most of them can be done in a few minutes with little or no planning. The only items used, if any, are classroom supplies such as paper and markers. The directions are simple and straightforward.

Exciting additions to *IceBreakers 3* are the tech tips for each activity, as well as a final chapter filled with tech IceBreaker games. The games have been successfully used in our ensemble rehearsals, music classes, faculty in-services, reading sessions, church choir practices and workshops. We believe we have a winning combination of ideas and are sharing our secret(s) of success with you.

In our teaching, we've realized that the life lessons taught on a daily basis are often the most important and are what students and audiences remember. If we do it right, we change hearts and lives forever. Teaching the heart in music provides breathtaking moments for the audience and performer alike. We do not remember the hours and hours in rehearsal…we remember moments! And you'll have plenty of moments to remember and capture with these fun IceBreaker activities.

Students today need to feel they belong and know they are an important and crucial part of the team. IceBreakers clear the way for learning by instantly bringing about conversation and making personal connections. These specific IceBreaker activities encourage the building of relationships as well as accepting and understanding differences. Use the games at the beginning of your classes and rehearsals. Students will hightail it into your room so they won't miss out on the fun. The games immediately involve the ensemble by shifting the focus from the teacher to the student from Day One. Your classes will never be the same!

So what are you waiting for? Let the games begin!

~*Valerie Lippoldt Mack* and *Matt Udland*

Special Note: We have provided specific names of web sites, apps, hardware, etc. just as examples, not endorsements. In many cases, there are multiple options to choose from, and you may already have a favorite you use. The world of technology is ever changing; if you can't find a tech solution we mention, ask us on Facebook, and we will be happy to help find a replacement!

In addition, several of our activities suggest taking photos of your students, posting pictures and text online, etc. You are the expert on what your district and school will allow, so please modify these suggestions as necessary and appropriate to address any established privacy guidelines.

MEET AND GREET
Introducing for the First Time

1. First Encounters of the Close Kind

Purpose

You get one chance to make a first impression; to be so awesome that no one can ignore you; to dress how you want to be addressed and act how you want to be treated. First impressions last forever. A little terrifying, isn't it? This exercise is a reminder that when you meet and greet, those first impressions will last a lifetime.

Directions

1. Display a current photo of a professional musician or band from a magazine, newspaper, poster or online photo.

2. Invite students to make comments based on first impressions. Look closely at the photo and the objects and/or people in the background. Is there agreement in the room on what type of impression is being given?

3. You get ONE chance to make a first impression. Discuss this idea. What are some ways your ensemble can make a good first impression? What impressions should NOT be given when first meeting someone? Why is this so important in the Arts? Do you agree with the statement, "You hear what a group looks like?" Is the visual as important as the aural?

Variations

Find photos over the years of your ensemble or photos from various school activities. What vibes are you picking up from these photos?

"Putting the SHOW in CHOIR!" another musical resource from Shawnee Press (35027799), introduces the idea of videotaping a portion of a rehearsal or class activity. First, ask students to watch the video without any sound. After focusing on the visual, turn off the picture and listen to the audio. Students will be surprised how much more intensely they will use the other senses and how they will notice little details with each of the assignments.

Tech Tips

Look at a group's web site or social media page, or for the brave, examine your own! If you have a secure online space where students can post to each other, post some photos into a discussion and have them comment on what they see, or have them make faces and adjust their posture for the perfect performance. Take a photo and post it online! How effective are they at portraying what you ask? Take a photo every day over a week with the group in their "perfect" performance posture. How did it change day to day? In 2016, the Mannequin Challenge exploded onto the social media scene! Walk through your "perfect posture" classroom while recording video and complete your own real-life mannequin challenge!

2. Break the Ice

Purpose

Students have the opportunity to practice moving around the room, staying very still, and using fun acting skills to get participants to "melt".

Directions

1. Students spread around the room and freeze in what they consider a "snowman pose."

2. One person (the Ice Sculptor) walks around with the goal of tricking a frozen snowman into wiggling. The Ice Sculptor cannot touch the snowman but CAN make faces, strike comical poses and make sounds of pretending to chisel away at a block of ice – anything to get the snowman to lose his or her cool and wiggle or break composure.

3. When the Ice Sculptor turns his back or isn't looking, the snowman can wiggle, make faces and blink, BUT if the Ice Sculptor catches the snowman in action, the snowman must immediately melt to the ground and stay seated the rest of the game.

4. Melted snowmen can enjoy the rest of the game by trying to assist the Ice Sculptor in melting their fellow snowmen.

Variations

I'm Melting … or Trying To! Give each student an ice cube. The goal is to melt the ice cube as quickly as possible – without putting it in your mouth! Decide if this is a partner or an individual activity, before the game begins!

Frozen T-Shirt: Unfold a frozen T-shirt and wear it. You can do this as a team or an individual race. Wet T-Shirt thoroughly, then put in a baggie in the freezer. Do whatever you need to do, to thaw out the T-shirt. First person to get the T-Shirt on is the winner.

Tech Tips

The worst part about being the Ice Sculptor in this game is missing all the hilarious faces and dance moves happening behind you. Clip a digital camera (such as a GoPro) onto the belt of the Ice Sculptor, facing behind them. Press record when the game starts, and you'll have hours of silly entertainment.

3. Self-Poetry Slam

Purpose

Creating self-descriptive poetry is a great way for students to embrace creativity and encourage deeper emotional sharing beyond surface-level questions.

Directions

1. Ask everyone in the class to sit down and think of a single sentence response to the following statements:

> I will forever _____,
> But I will never _____.
> I believe_____,
> and I am _____.

2. Each person should come up with a title for their poem, and recite it after introducing their name and the title of the poem.

Some students will take this very seriously and bare their souls, while others will be silly. Either way, everyone learns about each other and is given an opportunity to share.

Variation

Have people work together to create poetry slam-style commentary on topics they take seriously. The women in our collegiate concert choir did this activity (Topic: Celebrate what it is to be a woman) and read their answers in silhouette before the performance. It was meaningful for the performers and audience members alike. The addition of the poetry offered opportunities for self-discovery, as well as being a welcomed break from the standard concert format.

Tech Tips

If you want to collect these poems digitally, create a digital fill-in form (such as a Google Form, Typeform, or fillable PDF form) that allows short answer responses to be typed in, instead of the blanks shown in the sample above. Have each student submit their answer and then see if people can guess who belongs to which poem!

4. Opposites Attract

Purpose

Dig deeper by getting to know each other with this IceBreaker. Instead of saying "we are both in the band", agree OR disagree on your shared love for reggae music or '80s rock. You may be at opposite sides on some issues, but you will find that you agree on other things. Keep answers short as to avoid embarrassing comments or divulging too much information.

Directions

1. Participants create two circles (one outer and one inner). Begin this activity by shaking hands with a person from the other circle. The outer circle moves clockwise and the inner circle moves counter-clockwise. If numbers are not even, the teacher or accompanist can participate, or one person can monitor and stop and start the music.

2. When the music begins, students walk to the beat in a circular motion. When music stops, shake hands or "high five" the person directly across the circle.

3. Find one commonality with this partner and find one thing the two of you do NOT have in common.

4. Students finish both answers in 60 seconds and then move to the next person. This continues for as many rounds as needed.

Variations

Take a Stand: This favorite, yet simple game that can be found in *IceBreakers 1* (Shawnee Press 35010427). In this activity, participants feel comfortable and learn things about each other they might not have ever discovered otherwise. The students and the instructor identify when they connect and when they have opposite views. Two items are mentioned. Students stand on the right side of the room if they like the first item mentioned better and the other students stand on the left side if they like the second item mentioned the best. A list of ideas for this game is on the next page. No straddling the line. All students must take a stand! Stand for something or you'll fall for anything!

Tech Tips

Try letting your students choose the music they walk to. Use a playback app that will allow you to change the speed of the beat (such as TempoSlowMo). Start with a song everyone knows and loves, and use the app to increase tempo and make them jog around the circles!

30 "Take a Stand" Ideas

Students stand on the right or the left side of the room, depending on which item they like best. Choose 10-15 topics that work for your class. Ask students to brainstorm ideas to add to this list.

1. Wrestle a mountain lion or fight off a shark?

2. Dogs or cats?

3. Spend time with a best friend or be in a roomful of friends?

4. Watch Netflix or go to a movie theatre?

5. Early morning rehearsal or late night rehearsal?

6. Direct a show or star in a show?

7. Spend money or save money?

8. Participate in water activities or lie on a beach?

9. Use a planner or play it by ear?

10. Healthy smoothie or yummy milkshake?

11. Read the book first or see the movie first?

12. Watch a pro football game or play flag football?

13. Lose your hearing or lose your sight?

14. See a mouse in the house or a snake in the lake?

15. Take a cruise or help with a mission trip?

16. Eat chocolate-covered grasshopper or fried rattlesnake?

17. Follow the rules or stretch the rules?

18. Lose your phone for a week or your car for a month?

19. Take the ACT test or eat a bucket of spicy hot wings?

20. Watch a sunrise or sunset?

21. Vacation at Disney World® or New York City?

22. Cold pizza for breakfast or hot biscuits and gravy?

23. Disco or heavy metal?

24. Play in an orchestra or a band?

25. Play in a Jazz band or a marching band?

26. Have a noisy friend or a nosey friend?

27. Are you "out of the box" or "go with the flow"?

28. Sit by a campfire or on a towel by the pool?

29. Find your true love or win the 2 million-dollar lottery?

30. Take a quick shower or a long bath?

5. High Five Salutations

Purpose

Get people moving and communicating in ways they didn't know were possible. Students will be learning each other's names in a non-traditional way. Classes that participate physically, bond much quicker. This is a great way to reduce tension and anxiety. This game immediately involves everyone.

Directions

1. Students form a circle with ample space between each student. The further the circle is spread apart, the more challenging it becomes. You may use 8-20 participants.

2. Each student lifts right hand into high five position. The goal is for students to high five each other in one fluid motion. One step by each student is permissible but only one and not a stutter step. Stumbling or falling disqualifies the student.

3. When a hand is high-fived, the motion is passed on to the next person on the right.

4. If a person misses the high five, they are out until the next round. After high-fiving around the circle, everyone must take one step out to expand the circle and must now high five to the opposite direction.

5. The winners are the participants that make it through the fifth round of high fives!

Variation

Surname Salutation: As you reach to high five the person on the right, you simultaneously say his or her last name. This movement and repeating of their name cements it in your memory. The more times you say someone's name out loud, the more likely you are to remember his or her name.

Tech Tips

When students get "out," have them take over making sound effects for the game! They could use their mouths or download an app like "300+ Super Sound Box" that allows them to play a host of ridiculous sound effects! Careful, not all sounds might be approved for your age level.

6. Silent Line Drills

Purpose

From *IceBreaker 1,* the **"Silent Line Drill"** was a favorite. We've added a few twists and more examples. This activity definitely encourages students to feel comfortable with one another and their new environment as they learn about their classmates.

Directions

1. The instructor presents a topic and group members silently arrange themselves in order. Students cannot speak but must use body language, gestures and actions to try to depict their answer.

2. Time the activity to see how quickly this can be done.

3. When finished, check to see if students lined up correctly by having them state their name and their answer.

Example topics for **Silent Line Drills**

- Birthdate: find out who shares a birthday (month, day and year)
- Height: this helps with costuming or riser formation (shortest to tallest)
- Brag: one word that describes something you are proud of (alphabetically A to Z)
- Favorite app or game
- Pet's name (alphabetically A to Z)

Variations

This activity can be used competition-style by competing with each class for the fastest time, or by comparing times. If competing, use evenly-divided groups and create two straight lines. Use a variety of categories to determine which side can form a silent line the quickest. Allow students to construct their own categories. This allows students to discover commonalities and differences between their classmates.

Silent Singing: Stand in a line and start a well-known song. Play or sing the first 2 or 3 notes of the chosen song. The director will cut everyone off. Continue the song in your head. No humming aloud! When the director points at a person in the line, they will play their instrument or sing in the right key, the right place in the song – and the correct lyrics, if that applies. A few ideas for songs: a favorite nursery rhyme, popular song, carol, folk song, Broadway favorite, or a jazz standard. This is a great exercise for concentration and improving the inner ear.

Tech Tips

Don't forget that your smartphone has a built-in timer to use for stopwatch games. Time it down to the millisecond; students love to know EXACTLY how long it took!

7. What's Behind the Curtain?

Purpose

A friendly competition will quickly solidify classmates' names and other chosen facts, in a fun and game-show way. The surprise element makes this game work. Be ready for students to line up at the door every class period.

Directions

1. Divide the class into two equal groups, standing on opposite sides of an opened door. (Hopefully your door opens into your classroom. If not, you can do this in the hallway. Or, if the door in your room isn't positioned to allow two groups on either side of it when opened, you can use a curtain or another barrier.) One person from each team will step up to either side of the door, hiding behind so the two can't see each other.

2. The teacher will say "5,6,7,8" and the two opponents jump out from either side of the door.

3. Both race to see who can say the other person's name first. Whoever says it first is the winner and their team gains a point. These two people step to the end of the line and the next two people are ready to hide and then jump out and say names.

4. The game continues until everyone has had a chance to reveal names. This is a great way to quickly learn names as well as getting some physical activity.

Variations

Instead of saying first names, provide the option to find out other information including: last name, vocal part, instrument played, class in school or other pertinent information regarding your class.

This game will be a lifesaver for teachers at the beginning of the year. It will reinforce and solidify students' names, or whatever facts you need to remember about your class members.

Tech Tips

Make a video of participants saying the names of their opponents as quickly as they can. Look at the number of seconds to accurately pick a winner! Give extra points for great diction – you need to understand the names of everyone!

Need more practice? Record a two-second video of every person saying his or her name. Combine them all with an app like iMovie or Splice Video Editor and upload to your class web page so students can practice!

8. Letters Around the Room

Purpose

Students can't help but learn about each other with this diverse IceBreaker. The sky's the limit as to what you can learn about the class members' personalities. This is guaranteed to provide fun as students familiarize themselves with each other.

Directions

1. Designate different areas of the room for each letter of the alphabet, or put them in groups. For example, use the 4 corners of the room for these alphabet groups: A-G, H-M, N-S and T-Z.

2. The instructor asks a question. The students are to stand together under the letter that starts with their answer. If the question is "What is your middle name?" and the answer is "Patrick", that individual would stand in the "P" area.

3. After students have assembled into these letter areas, they share their answers. In this case they would share middle names.

4. Once everyone has shared, the instructor asks another question. Here are some sample topics. (Use the first letter of your answer to find your area.)

   - Favorite school mascot
   - Nickname
   - Favorite ice cream topping
   - Free time activity
   - Place you shop in the mall
   - Single pizza flavor
   - Scariest type of weather/storm
   - Type of candy you could eat for a week
   - Childhood Halloween costume
   - What do or did you call your grandparents?
   - What superhero are you most like?
   - Best advice you ever received

Variations

If you have a big group, keep each alphabet letter separate. If you have a smaller group of students, you can group together letters of the alphabet.

Tech Tips

Keep a spreadsheet of the information you get from this. Even an audio recording of answers can be helpful later! If you had a recording or list of everyone's favorite candy, you could use it for simple and thoughtful rewards. Students won't believe you remembered!

9. Zoom Around the Room

Purpose

Zoom around the room, or just spin in a circle! This IceBreaker gets students moving, encourages them to learn each other's names, and instills the confidence to look into the eyes of their peers!

Directions

1. Students stand and form a circle.

2. When instructed, students run eight steps to the right, looking ahead while repeating "**Zoom**" and clapping (8 times). Shout the name of a member in the circle on count 9 and at the same time, jump and look at that person's face.

3. If two people end up shouting each other's names at the same time, both people must sit down until the next round.

Disclaimer: If a player doesn't say a name or makes up a name of someone not in the circle, they will be disqualified and need to wait until the next round to participate.

Variations

This variation is played using the phrase *"2, 4, 6, 8, who do we appreciate? I see YOU!"* Students can put arms around each other's shoulders and run in a circle. They look up as they freeze on the last syllable (YOU!). If two people DO make eye contact with each other, they sit down and wait for the next round. Whoever is left standing is the declared winner. This works best if done with a circle of 8-16 people.

Tech Tips

To keep these games in tempo, use a metronome (or metronome app!) and put an 8-count rest in-between rounds. This gives the people that are "out," time to step out of the circle. This way, there is no time to argue or discuss the results. Keeping in time reinforces tempo and adds an element of urgency to the exercise. Start slowly and steadily increase the tempo.

Once your class is comfortable with each other, break out a phone or camera and have them snap a picture of the person they are looking at when they turn around! You'll get some funny photos, and it should be very easy to tell if students did in fact catch each other in the act!

RACES AND RELAYS

Physical Activities for the Team

10. Awkward 8-Count

Purpose

This activity works for choreographed ensembles, vocal jazz (scatting) and instrumental students as a silly and fun IceBreaker. There are bigger rewards by the time the exercise is finished! Students should not feel embarrassed or self-conscious when performing this exercise. Rather, use the awkwardness and have fun. It is much easier to perform this in a smaller setting. Allow the process to help the performer grow and not feel humiliated on stage or in front of a larger group. It may take several rounds but remember – practice makes perfect.

Directions

1. Construct circles of eight to ten students.

2. Each volunteer has 8 counts to move to the center of the circle and share an awkward 8-count dance. The sillier the dance, the better.

3. This exercise, even though it seems utterly ridiculous, is actually the thing needed to get students to create something – musically or choreographically. This is a chance to perform (and yet not on the stage) in a small way that will lead to more confidence on stage. Small steps.

Variations

Awkward Scenario: create various awkward scenarios for small groups to act out for the rest of the class.

- You didn't get the lead in the school musical after telling friends you had it in the bag.
- You are the drum major and at the football halftime, you get off beat and confused in front of the home crowd.
- Boy/girlfriend breaks up with you in the middle of your music class.
- Cool person says "hey" to you and you respond, only to find they were talking to someone else on their phone.
- You have a wardrobe malfunction as you walk out on stage.
- You accidentally call your music teacher "mom".

Tech Tips

Over time, this exercise can turn into a quality way for students to practice improvisation. Consider creating some music loops (using an app like GarageBand) for students to improv to. Choose a song with a strong beat, no vocals and predictable chord progressions to help them step outside their comfort zone.

11. Dancing Cell Phone

Purpose

In the old version of "Telephone," students would whisper one word or phrase and pass it around the circle. It was a bit like "gossip" because the phrase that first started around the circle rarely ends up the same – as it does in real-life gossip. This game has a new twist. Literally!

Directions

1. Students stand in a circle. The starter of the game taps the person next to them and performs one "dance phrase" with just that person watching. This game is exactly like "telephone" but is done with an 8-count of dance instead of whispering a phrase.

2. Everyone else keeps their head down and eyes shut until it is their turn.

3. The 2nd person watches the 8-count dance phrase and then they tap the person next to them so they can watch the 8-ct.

4. This continues until each person has participated. The student cannot repeat the move. The goal is to get the dance moves as close as possible to the original.

Variations

Funny Face Phone: The leader makes a funny face and passes it on to the next person and so on. It is important to take a photo at the beginning so you can compare faces. Hide your face from others so only the person next to you can see!

Silent Cell Phone: The leader mouths a made-up phrase and passes it down. The last person in the circle says it out loud at the same time as the leader that made up the phrase. How well do you all read lips?

Body Stomp Phone: One person makes a sound with body percussion. The next person repeats that and adds on. Repeat until someone can't remember. You can help the person OR start the game over, depending how competitive you decide to be. You can also compete in two straight lines. Ideas for sounds: Stomp, stamp, slap, clap, snap, click tongue, sniff, slap cheeks, click tongue, kissing sound, smack lips, click heels, click toes. Beginning students should be given a set amount and keep it simple (clap, stomp, snap, slap). To make it easier, give fewer sound choices.

Tech Tips

Video the dance at the beginning and at the end of the game. Simply share the videos with the class so they can see how it changed or edit them together so they can view them later. Videos give ownership and create great opportunities for quick writing blogs or discussions.

12. Musical Body Parts

Purpose

Students interact with each other while enjoying music in a non-threatening environment. This is a fun way to meet others since everyone is doing embarrassing things at the same time. Students will soon feel comfortable moving to the music and trying to react in a split second. Caution: this exercise WILL result in laughter!

Directions

1. When music starts, the instructor announces a number followed by a certain body part. It is the students' job to find the right number of body parts and people(s) to connect with as quickly as possible. Examples:

   - 25 toes
   - 7 elbows
   - 3 knees
   - 2 heads
   - 4 hips
   - 33 fingers
   - 2 cheeks
   - 3 ears
   - 5 wrists
   - 4 noses

2. Once the music stops, see how everyone did! Encourage students to participate so they don't miss out on this great team building exercise. If students need more incentive to participate, award points for being most creative, most inclusive, and fastest.

Variations

For a fun variation, use items found in backpacks or the classroom instead of body parts! This will help create a physical buffer in this exciting and high-energy IceBreaker.

Tech Tips

Search online for free spinner tools that allow you to create your own digital wheel. Let students spin the wheel. Everyone will be surprised with the musical body parts that are announced. Teachers can't be accused of trying to "fix" a game. The Wheel will decide!

Games where you need to yell out numbers or objects over laughing students can become frustrating if everyone can't hear you. If you don't have a microphone but have a stereo with a line-in port, you can use your phone as a megaphone! Apps like Megaphone Free send what you say into the mic out through the headphone port. Now you have a quick mic for those loud IceBreakers!

13. Snake-in' Around

Purpose

Students interact with each other in a non-threatening environment. This activity gives students a chance to exercise and maneuver around obstacles on a different level – literally!

Directions

1. The player declared "number one snake" lies down on the ground on his or her stomach.

2. Everybody else gathers fearlessly around to touch the "snake". One toe will suffice. Who wants to touch a snake anyway!?

3. When music begins, everybody tiptoes, staying within the bounds of the snake area, while the snake, moving on his or her belly, tries to tag as many as he can. Those touched, become snakes as well. Untagged players run bravely around in the snake-infested area, trying to avoid being caught. The atmosphere gets even better if all the snakes are hissing.

4. The last person caught is the starter snake in the next game.

Variations

Don't be Crabby! The game is played the same as above except everyone is walking on their hands and feet in a crab position. All claws (hands and feet) are considered fair game to tag another person.

Bear with Me: Walk on hands and feet in a "bear" position.

Wheelin' and Dealin': This is a partner exercise with one holding the feet of their partner, as in a "wheel barrow," while the other person uses their hands to walk around the room.

Cradle Catch: Two lines face each other and one person is in a cradle catch (like a baby). Pass the babies down the line – cradle to cradle – and feet can't touch the floor. First baby to the end of the line is the winning team.

Blind Mice: Put coats or scarves over the students' eyes for this variation. Students can make squeaking noises but can't open eyes. Students will improve listening skills from this silly sightless activity.

Tech Tips

Students can get very good at these kinds of games. If you want to make it a bit more challenging, try shutting the lights low and have them use their phone flashlights to see the snakes!

14. Volume Up!

Purpose

Understanding dynamics in music is the purpose of this activity. All students contribute by moving and acting out various dynamic levels. One variation allows the students to see the dynamic symbol on the board and to physically demonstrate the dynamic with their body.

Directions:

1. Here is a game to reinforce the musical concept of moving from *piano* to *forte*. If you don't believe that this concept needs to be learned, just think how many times you've had to ask a child to use his or her "inside voice."

2. Choose a word or phrase that is fun to say and repeat the word over and over. For example: fuddy duddy, gibberish, wishy-washy, snicker doodle, or use lyrics from a song and repeat with increasing dynamics.

3. The teacher and the class say the word starting softly, squatting on the floor, arms at your side. As the volume increases, gradually stand up and end up on tiptoes while raising your arms up to the sky. Then reverse the exercise by adding a gradual *decrescendo* as you repeat the phrase, ending in a tight little ball on the floor.

Variations

Take your students back to the '80s and have them pretend to turn a boom box volume dial as they get loud and soft. Crank the music up and back down quickly. This is a fun and effective way to teach the amplification of sound and dynamics.

Master a steady *crescendo* and *decrescendo*. Try holding up fingers and have the students change volume according to that number. 1 is pianissimo; 10 is fortissimo. Change the numbers from high to low and in between to practice fast dynamic changes.

List random dynamic markings on a whiteboard. One person points at the dynamic marking on the board and students need to immediately demonstrate the constantly changing louds and softs with their bodies. Don't forget *crescendos, decrescendos, ppp, mp, mf, fff, sfz, sffz, accents, subito, piano, forte, fortissimo, mezzo-forte*. Use both words and signs to increase and reinforce learning.

Tech Tips

Sometimes, especially when explaining to very young students, it is best to demonstrate your desired outcomes. Choose a song they know, and have students associate dynamic levels with the proper musical terms while adjusting the volume knob higher and lower.

15. Head, Shoulders, Knees...Say What?!?

Purpose:

This game works on many levels. Students sing *a cappella*, get physical exercise as they are reaching head to toes and get an opportunity to share a part of their life. If they volunteer to share a story, they have the chance to share personal experiences. If they choose to listen, they are learning about their classmates.

Directions

1. Sing and act out the silly tune of "Head, Shoulders, Knees and Toes." The second section of the song is "Eyes and ears and mouth and nose", then repeats back to the first phrase of "Head, Shoulders, Knees and Toes."

2. Whenever the instructor raises his or her hand, the class must freeze.

3. One person volunteers to tell a story that reminds them of that body part. Of course, this game won't work for all classes.

   ### Ideas:

   Head – the time I was headstrong and made a big purchase without thinking

   Shoulders – a favorite choreographed move involving the shoulders

   Knees – I remember hurting my knee playing football in 5th grade

   Toes – the pedicure I had with my mom

   Eyes – the first time I tried to put in contacts

   Ears – my dad is a Husker fan (ears of corn)

   Mouth – I've never had a cavity

   Nose – my allergies are really bad this year

Variations

Heads or Tails: Flip a coin. As the coin is being tossed in the air, students grab their head or their "tails" and freeze in this silly pose. The coin toss is won if the student is grabbing the correct part of the body as the coin is called. If the student is wrong, they sit down. If right, keep playing until one winner remains.

Awesome Alphabet: As a class, sing the alphabet. When the leader points at a player, everyone stops singing. The chosen player shares a positive sentiment that begins with the same letter.

Tech Tips

I can't remember the last time I had a coin in my pocket … but a smartphone or tablet is almost always in reach. Use an app like Coin Flip when you are out of change. If you don't want to download an app, try asking your phone's voice assistant to flip one for you!

16. Animal Signs

Purpose

This game strengthens coordination, memory, teamwork and creativity. Most importantly, students will act like animals and have a whole lot of fun!

Directions

1. Start in a circle of 3-10 people and assign each person an animal and corresponding hand action.

2. One player starts by slapping legs, clapping, slapping legs, and executing the action of their assigned animal. Repeat the slap pattern and make the animal action of the next animal (person) that you want to follow you.

3. The 2nd person slaps legs, claps, slaps legs, executes their animal action and then slap, clap, slap, another animal action (whomever they pass the game to).

4. This is a silent game. Leave the circle when you can't remember your animal action.

   - Moose – jazz hands to both sides of head to represent horns
   - Rooster – 1 jazz hand wiggles on the top of head to form the rooster comb
   - Dog – both hands curl over to create paws
   - Unicorn – index finger to top of head to form a unicorn horn
   - Cow – jazz hands to tummy makes the cow udder
   - Elephant – one hand stretches out long by nose to form trunk
   - Raccoon – hands form circles around eyes to make "raccoon eyes"
   - Bird – bent wrists by shoulders to create wings
   - Bear – hands turn into claws
   - Fish – make fish face and hands become gills on sides of face
   - Rabbit – 2 fingers up by ears to make rabbit ears
   - Alligator – arms out front and clap like alligator jaws
   - Shark – elbows bend in and clap together like jaws
   - Duck – fingers "quack" at mouth
   - Gorilla – fists beat on chest
   - Chicken – elbows wiggle like in the chicken dance

Variations

Class can create more animal actions, if there are more people in the circle. Try this turbo speed for a real challenge.

Tech Tips

This game is something we use the first week of our classes! If you want to see it in action so you understand how much fun it is, visit the Butler Vocal Music Facebook page. Recorded in 360 degrees, these animal signs and a few more will be demonstrated by Butler music students.

17. Goal ... Jazz Hands

Purpose

Here is an exercise to see how someone can convince you to do something. Do you listen and reason, or just conform to fit in? Brute force, bullying, tickling, bribery, deceitfulness, insincerity, double-dealing and untruthfulness are ways to accomplish this activity. Try this IceBreaker and see how you fare.

Directions

1. Pair up students. Be sure the teacher does this, so students are matched up fairly and equally.

2. Announce that you are timing students to see who can first open their partner's fists and turn fingers into two jazz hands.

3. Give students exactly one minute to execute the exercise. If anyone makes a noise or says stop, both students are out until next time.

4. When the game is over, discuss the tactics and the results. How many tried to use force to open the fist? Who tried to talk their way to a solution? How many tried to bribe? Anyone try to come up with a compromise? Is there any way this could be a win, win situation?

Variations

Toe Overboard: If a person can convince his partner to step over an imaginary line, they win the round. You cannot touch your partner. This game is similar to *"Red Rover, Red Rover"* but instead of running through a line, students can smooth talk their way to win. When the game is over, analyze the results. Did students talk out of turn? Were people reacting how you expected? Did anyone discover they could carry someone else's partner over the line? But be careful, both are disqualified if one of the partners yells "Toe Overboard!"

Tech Tips

Choose one person to take photos of this game in action! Post to a worksheet or forms service like Wizer or Typeform, both of which are free for teachers, and vote for the most creative methods. Have a meme contest! Make sure to always discuss proper online social etiquette before asking students to share. We remind students they are representing us online as much as themselves. If they wouldn't say it to our face, they shouldn't say it online!

18. Bust a Move and Name it!

Purpose

This thought-provoking group activity will stretch the student's ability using teamwork and will also eliminate self-consciousness. Students enjoy having a move named after them and feel significant that they made a contribution in this physical IceBreaker.

Directions

1. Divide students into smaller groups, making sure groups are divided equally considering talent. There is a five-minute time limit for this activity.

2. Instructors can have a song selected or use time before the exercise to let the class vote on a song.

3. Make up a dance step, or a short combination, as a group and name the dance move.

4. Each group gets a turn to teach their original choreography to the rest of the class. If several sections of choreography are pieced together, the class will have choreographed an entire song. This is a fun thing to do from time to time, but if done as a regular activity, it could waste valuable rehearsal and turn into a stressor instead of a fun IceBreaker.

Variations

Bust a Riff: What kind of fun sounds can you make? Can others repeat?

Bust an Impression: Can you imitate a famous person and nail it? Can you be so good that others can guess who you are? Teachers are fair game – but NOT students in (or out!) of the room.

Bust a Pose: The instructor will give partners 20 seconds to come up with an amazing pose. Most students will try to do some type of lift or will be silly with a partner. Be sure the room has adequate space – AND carpet!

Bust a Rap: Pass a rap around the room and see how long you can keep the rap going. Pick a subject and have people volunteer to join in. The rest of the room is keeping a steady beat.

Tech Tips

Not everyone can be a YouTube sensation, BUT videotaping and sharing your creation is the first step to gaining free publicity for your group!

LISTEN AND LEARN

2 Ears, 2 Eyes and 1 Mouth in Proper Proportion

19. Listen! OK?

Purpose

Listening is an important factor in building good relationships. It is essential for good communication – and that helps students interact effectively with each other. If you want better ensemble work, learn to "Listen! OK?"

Directions

1. This game can be played various times during class. It is a riddle and clues are given if you "listen" carefully. Some students will catch on quicker than others. That may frustrate, but also motivate students to solve the game. Don't share the answer, as it is more fun to "earn the right to play!"

2. The instructor says "OK, I can play the Knock on Wood game. Can you play the Knock on Wood game?" Then the instructor knocks on nearby wood.

3. IF the student understands how the game is played, he will listen for the word "OK" that is said before the sentence. The knocking on wood has nothing to do with the game. Most students will concentrate and watch where and how the instructor knocks on wood.

4. If the student doesn't start the sentence with "OK, I can play the Knock on Wood game," they don't understand the riddle and need to try again.

Variations

"Jammin' James jumped, did he jump?" Now listen! The answer is "yes" IF the person starting the game begins the sentence with "Now listen!" If they don't start the sentence with "Now listen!" the answer is "no." Again, once you understand the game, it is really fun to watch others that are trying to understand the game. It is a great "a ha!" moment when someone cracks the code.

Tech Tips

Play variations of this game with large groups of people by creating QR codes for assessment. For example, an app like Plickers lets you poll your class for free, without the need for student devices. Plickers creates a QR code for each student. Each unique QR code can be rotated to represent different responses. Starting the sentence with a different word requests a different response, such as "Are you ready to play? (A)" "But you don't look ready. (B) Can't you figure it out? (C) or "Do you understand what is going on? (D). Hold up your smartphone and point it at the class. Instead of having class members respond verbally, have them rotate their plicker card to hold up "A/B/C/D" to respond. Plickers is perfect for small ensembles or groups of less than 63 people and can be used for quick formative assessment during almost any learning activity.

20. Sounds Good to Me...

Purpose

Students will listen for the timbre of a sound and the location of where the sound was created. Sounds easy? Go for it!

Directions

1. The class can sit and put their heads down on desks. If desks are not available, they can sit on the floor or on risers. Ask students to close their eyes.

2. The instructor secretly selects five students. Those five students quietly spread around the room. They will make a MUSICAL sound with some item in the room. If the room is empty, body percussion is allowed.

3. To answer, you must guess the sound and where the sound is coming from. Whoever guesses correctly gets to be one of the next sound leaders.

Ideas for Creating Musical Sounds

- Pitch pipe
- Pluck piano string
- Buzz a mouthpiece
- Scratch fingernails on a chalkboard
- Drop coins on a desk
- Slam a book shut
- Turn a light switch on and off
- Scoot a chair on the floor
- Tap pencil on the floor
- Slap knees, clap hands, snap fingers, stomp the floor
- Smack lips

Variations

7 is the Magic Number: Have students sing a chromatic scale but using numbers 1, 2, 3 up to 12 and then end on *do* (1). Singing down the chromatic scale starts 1, 12, 11, 10 and back to one. Split the group in half and ½ of the room sings *a cappella* 1 up to 12 and finishes on 1. The other half sings down the scale 1, 12, 11 and ends on 1. If the groups sing ½ steps correctly, everyone meets at "7" in the middle on a unison note. This is great aural exercise for vocal and instrumental musicians.

Tech Tips

If you don't have anything in your room to make noise, try playing sound effects from a phone! A variety of free apps are available, or you could create a set of sounds for them to identify using a web site like www.soundboard.com.

21. And the Point Is...

Purpose

Communication – verbal and nonverbal – is vital to every organization. If a leader can't get a point across clearly and motivate others, then the message doesn't matter. Learn how much influence one "leader" can or can't have.

Directions

1. Form circles of 10-20 participants. The instructor becomes the first "pointer" (#1) of the game and starts the game by pointing at another person (#2) in the circle.

2. Person #2 now points at another person (#3) and so on until everyone is pointing at one person and has a person pointing at them. Whoever finishes the first round will be pointing at the instructor (#1).

3. Once the order is established, everyone quits pointing but continues staring at their selected person.

4. Stand as still as possible. The instructor will make a small movement. Students need to stay focused on only one person.

5. Everyone imitates the movement exactly and then freezes. Play the game until everyone understands the point… to become more focused!

Variations

Point or Grab: Stand in a circle and reach arms out. Face your left palm up and point your right index finger down into the palm of the neighbor's left palm. The instructor says "Point" or "Grab". If the word "point" is said, nothing happens. If the word "grab" is said, students try to grab neighbor's pointing right index finger with their left hand while protecting their right finger from being grabbed. The fun part is the suspense of not knowing when the "grab" word will come. The instructor could shout "great," "grasp," "go" or other words similar to "grab" to make sure everyone is listening. **And the point is…** students must listen carefully or mistakes are made. (Note: this variation is best used with older students, who will know not to grab fingers too aggressively!)

Tech Tips

Someone could play a low E and F back and forth, gradually getting faster, to create some suspenseful music. If you don't have a piano, use a Virtual Piano app on a mobile device!

22. Circle Taps

Purpose

This sensory game seems simple, but students will be surprised how challenging "Circle Taps" can be. Comical chaos is sure to ensue as team members concentrate on one hand and the other hand may accidentally respond. This game takes attention, eye-hand coordination and dexterity. Entertainment will definitely be provided for those watching the circle of tapping hands!

Directions

1. Sit in a circle with hands on the table, crossing wrists – right wrist on top of left wrist.

2. Starting with the leader, tap one time on a hand of the person next to you. The leader can decide which direction to send the taps. Each player continues the tap around the circle with one tap. If someone double taps, the tapping direction reverses.

3. If you make a mistake or take longer than 3 seconds to respond you must remove your hands from the circle.

4. The game can speed up as participants feel more confident.

Variations

Electricity: Divide the class into equal lines of 15-20 people. Hold hands, shut eyes and get ready to feel the electricity from one person to the next. An impartial person (generator) stands at the end of the lines and holds hands with both leaders from the two lines. The "generator" starts the electricity by squeezing at the same time, the hands of the first people in line. The "electricity" (squeezing) moves from one person to the next. Once it arrives at the end of the line, reverse the electricity back down the line, back to the "generator". Whichever hand is squeezed first, that line is declared the winning team. If the electricity skips and the flow of the electric charge misses a person, the line must start completely over with the generator.

Tech Tips

Using our hands backwards is complicated, even for students who treat their phone like an extension of their fingers. Give students a sentence and have them try to text it to you quickly using only their less dominant hand. The autocorrect alone will create some fun responses.

23. Tightrope Tiptoe

Purpose

This is an exercise in which the participant must concentrate. It teaches the individual to trust throughout the process. Students may be nervous when they close their eyes, but the participants are totally secure as the game is completely risk-free. It is the thought of falling that makes the student feel vulnerable.

Directions

1. Have students evenly divide and line up on opposite sides of the room, ready to walk a pretend tightrope.

2. Turn off the lights and ask students to keep their eyes shut on the honor system. This makes the exercise more exciting and complete. For a large class, create multiple lines so many students are participating at the same time.

3. One student per line reaches arms to the sides and pretends to walk across a Highwire. As the person walks, the player across the divide uses vocal cues to guide them safely. When the tightrope walker finishes tiptoeing across the pretend chasm, their guide reaches for their hands to help stop their journey.

4. The guide is now ready to shut his or her eyes and cross the Highwire back to original side. It sounds crazy, but removing one of your senses to cross the room takes bravery!

Variations

Trust Walk: The instructor pairs students together. One is assigned to be the leader and the other, the trusting follower. If blindfolds are not available, put a hoodie over the eyes or keep eyes shut. The trust walk can take place around the classroom, on a stage or outdoors. Spin the person around a couple of times for more suspense. The guiding partner will steer the trusting partner away from obstacles. The guide will be challenged by taking care and being responsible for another person and the trusting partner must of course, trust.

Trust Fall: A person stands in the middle of the circle with eyes closed and arms crossed. The "middle trusting person" falls deliberately in various directions and trusts the rest of the group to catch him and push him back to standing position before he falls again. Don't do this activity unless you have plenty of spotters and trust for everyone involved.

Tech Tips

A quick search for "Silly Circus Music" on YouTube will help set the mood for your tightrope acts! If you want to add an element of suspense and change the mood, change the music. The atmosphere will immediately transform. That is the amazing power of music!

24. Ice, Ice Breaker

Purpose

Students can try to rap some of their serious choral pieces or select a well-known tune. The hard part is that the rap is done in silence. This "Read My Lips" game is a fun twist and makes students watch carefully while giving the lips and the mouth quite a workout. The by-product of this IceBreaker is that diction and embouchures will improve. Performers will be more comfortable with the use of facial expressions in front of larger audiences.

Directions

1. Students decide on a phrase in a song and mouth one line of the song in a rap style.

2. How quickly can the rest of the class figure out what song and what exactly was mouthed? Many people communicate through lip-reading and clear communication is extremely important on stage. This is a great exercise to work on diction, as well a facial warm-up.

3. Whoever guesses correctly is the next person to be the Ice, Ice Breaker.

Variations

Mouth a Mood: Divide into two teams. One at a time, a person mouths a mood or an emotion to their team. Take turns as team members act out what mood they think was mouthed by the leader.

- Anger
- Disgust
- Happiness
- Sadness
- Surprise
- Fear
- Hopeful
- Anxious
- Confused
- Embarrassed
- Guilty
- Jealous
- Proud
- Courageous

Vowel Mood: This is a simple trick taught to us by John Jacobson. Want a quick facial warm up? Say the five vowels and overdo your facials on each vowel. Invite one half of the class to perform the vowels and the other half looks for the most overdone vowels. Switch and let the others perform the five vowels. Then, it's the instructor's turn!

Tech Tips

A teacher could post a video without sound, mouthing a line of a song and send it to students. First student to respond to the post/text wins! Sharing in a secure online space where students can respond to each other about what it looked like can be really fun!

25. 4'33"

Purpose

Listening is not the same as hearing. Listening requires a focus not present in just hearing. Listening is key to being able to effectively communicate. Being able to repeat what was communicated is key to better interaction in the classroom. A good listener listens to what is said, but also to the silence.

Directions

1. Describe or play a recording of John Cage's **4'33"** composition. Even though it was written in 1952, the piece is still relevant today. It consists of the sounds of the environment that the listeners hear while it is performed. As a result when listening to the piece, the audience becomes more focused.

2. Have students sit outside in the hallway, outside on a nature hike, or even in another classroom. Get ready for focused listening.

3. Students repeat verbally what they heard in the four minutes and 33 seconds.

4. After listening, can the students recreate the piece? Of course, they wouldn't be able to do exactly, but how close can they come to reconstructing the piece.

Variations

Read and discuss these ideas about listening. Do you agree or disagree? "You learn as much if not more from listening than from performing." "Most of the time we don't really listen. We only pretend to listen so we can respond and hear ourselves talk." "Hearing happens. Listening is something you have to concentrate and do consciously." "The brain has to be engaged for listening. Hearing is an involuntary process." Have students create some instances when they are listening or when they are simply hearing something.

Are there procedures to guarantee an exciting composition? How much does the audience contribute to this piece? How much does the audience contribute overall during other performances? Is that a good or bad thing?

Tech Tips

Listening is so important for groups to be able to communicate clearly. Describing what you hear can be difficult. Try recording soundscapes and playing them back. Participants can discuss what they hear using musical terms. There is also a 4'33" app that helps you create and share your own production.

26. Number Shout Out!

Purpose

Learn to focus as a team. Learn to listen and be patient as members try to count without stepping on anyone else's number. Play this game several times in a row, working to reach a higher number and set a record.

Directions

1. Students can sit, stand or even lie down on the floor. Once in place, students shut their eyes. One person is always the leader and starts by saying "one."

2. Students randomly shout out numbers in succession. (1,2,3,4,5...) However, if two people chime in and say a number at the same time, the game starts completely over with the first person saying "one" again.

3. See if the group can come up with a plan, so don't give advance directions. Do any leaders stand out by trying to lead in a positive manner?

4. Secret tip: the faster you go, the easier it is.

5. To keep the game interesting, switch leaders every so often.

Variations

Sing Out Solfège: Try this game using solfège by singing the pitch (up and down) for music variation. Once you've reached the octave *do*, come back down the scale.

Shout Out to Musical Words: Instead of saying numbers, try spelling various musical words. For an **advanced variation,** don't supply the word, and the group doesn't get to discuss. To play, one person begins with the first letter and then see what musical word comes out of the process. Higher level of thinking is used for sure!

Tech Tips

Ringtone Roulette: Get out cell phones and go to alarm or ringtone settings. Try to get everyone in the room to play a ringtone. The ringtones can't be the same AND they can't play at the same time.

Name that Ringtone: Can you guess which ringtone belongs to which person? If so, point at the person and shout it out!

27. Tongue Twisting Turmoil

Purpose

Speaking is probably the most complex motor activity we do. Getting the brain to coordinate the lips, tongue, jaw and larynx is quite a challenge. Listening is the ability to receive and interpret messages. To get these two things to work together is quite an accomplishment. Good listening and speaking skills will lead to a more productive rehearsal. Everyone benefits – and all students have a fun time trying to recite the tongue twisters!

Directions

1. The instructor speaks one of the tongue twisters from the list below. The class tries to repeat the tongue twister five times, as fast as possible, collectively.

2. The instructor randomly selects a student to repeat the selected tongue twister.

3. If the student successfully pronounces the tongue twister, she gets to choose the next tongue twister of the day. If she struggles, another person can offer to step in and help.

Ideas for Tongue Twisters:

Three free throws, low roller lower roller, big black bug, freshly-fried flying fish, pirates private property, black bug's blood, selfish shellfish, knapsack straps, shredded Swiss cheese, six sticky sucker sticks, Mrs. Smith's fish sauce shop, Irish wrist-watch, daddy draws doors, eleven benevolent elephants, one smart fellow he felt smart (not for middle school boys!)

Toughest Tongue Twister of all time? The sixth sick sheikh's sixth sheep's sick. Try saying it six times in succession! We dare you!

For more great tongue twisting ideas, check out Greg Gilpin's *"115 Tang Tungling Tongue Twisters from A to Z!"* (35027638). This is an invaluable vocal warm-up resource from Shawnee Press.

Variations

Give students extra credit for inventing new tongue twisters. Give a prize at the end of the year for the students' choice tongue twister.

Tech Tips

Want to test diction? Record the winner and play it for a person who doesn't know what they are supposed to be saying. Could also use an online digital assistant (such as Siri, Cortana, OK Google, or Amazon Echo) and see if it could understand you!

28. Class Trip

Purpose

These brainteaser-type games (must) use reasoning and logical thinking. The team must brainstorm and work together to solve the riddle. This exercise can be used on numerous occasions during the year – until everyone is "on" the Class Trip!

Directions

1. The teacher begins by creating a list of words with double consonants and then asking, "Who can join me on the Class Trip? I'm taking the Basses but not Tenors on the Class Trip. I could take jazz singers, but not the Chamber Choir on the Class Trip. I could also take ballerinas, mezzos, cellos, drummers, and professionals."

2. The student that figures out the double consonant theme is allowed on the "Class Trip." Students must keep trying until they figure out the riddle!

Variations

Abbreviated Trip: Valerie Mack is going on a band trip and taking a vacuum and a magic wand. Matt Udland is taking a mitt and an umbrella. Who wants to go? Students catch on if they think of items that start with the letter of their first and last names.

Triple Trip: I'm going on a bus tour and taking a dog, a cat and a cow, but won't be taking a puppy, a kitten or a calf. You figure out the riddle if you take items that have three letters.

Spirited Trip: I'm going on a school trip and point at objects in the room. Can I take this and this and this and this? The answer is yes for the next object after the leader points at something with school colors or a school mascot. Otherwise, the answer is no.

Magical Musical Trip: The person guessing and the person giving the clues are really in cahoots, but the rest of the class shouldn't be aware of this fact. The guesser steps out of the room and the class decides on an object. The guesser comes back in the room and the clue giver begins pointing at all kinds of things in the room. The magic is that whatever item is pointed to AFTER a musical item is the item the class chose. The guesser will appear to be "magical." The goal is to see if any of the class members can join the "Magical Musical Trip."

Tech Tips

Some riddles might take too long to figure out in class. Try messaging a riddle to the class over a long weekend to keep students engaged with you when they are away. First to get the correct answer back to you wins!

29. Listen and Learn

Purpose

The old saying, "do as I say, not as I do" does NOT apply for this game. Instead, this activity is designed to help students improve listening skills. If students have difficulty following directions, they can become lost and overwhelmed during class-guided activities. Students will improve their listening ability with this simple IceBreaker.

Directions

1. Students are instructed to spread out in the room and shut their eyes.

2. The leader gives several physical directions for the students to execute. The students continue to keep their eyes shut as they perform the commands.

3. Ideas for Listen and Learn

   - Turn and face the back of the room
   - Place right hand over head
   - Move left hand parallel to the floor
   - Pick up right knee and put in tree position (passé)
   - Tilt head to the left
   - Flip wrists up
   - Bend left knee and freeze

4. After all these commands, students are instructed to open their eyes. Are they all in the same body position?

5. Are students listening and hearing the same things? Why or why not? How can students improve their listening skills?

Variations

Swingin' Around: Two leaders choose partners and swing them around several times. Carefully let go of your partner's hands and watch the partners spin out of control. The goal of this game is to see who can freeze first and hold the pose the longest – and without making a sound. No screaming allowed! For dancers, this is a great exercise in learning to spot when turning, as well as working on staying in control.

Tech Tips

This is a really fun game to see in fast motion. Set up a phone on a tripod or have someone hold it and use an app such as Hyperlapse to record a time-lapse video. It'll look like a fast-paced dance when you are done!

30. Applause, Applause!

Purpose

Students will fight distraction and focus on the subject at hand. Your class will learn to concentrate for a period of time and quickly judge content in a musical topic. When that happens, be sure to applaud them!

Directions

1. The teacher will select and share one musical category, and then list several words that belong in this category, and one word that doesn't belong.

2. Students clap if the word belongs in the category and snap if it doesn't. The teacher will read the items quickly as to keep the game moving and for more applause. This allows the instructor to see if students understand what is going on. This activity can be a fun IceBreaker-type game and it checks knowledge in a given area.

   ### Ideas for Categories

   - Brass Instruments
   - Christmas Carols
   - Marching Band Compositions
   - Orchestral Composers
   - Broadway Musicals
   - Tempo Markings
   - Woodwind Instruments
   - Dynamic Markings
   - Famous Operas
   - Country Music Artists
   - Classical Music Greats
   - Vocal Jazz Standards

Variations

Clap and Echo Game: The leader claps a selected pattern for four counts. The rest of the class repeats the four counts while the leader continues creating new rhythm patterns. The leader will be clapping a new pattern while the rest of the class responds with the four counts, echoing the pattern.

Tech Tips

Assess knowledge quickly by having the class text answers back to you, or use a free group chat forum (such as todaysmeet.com) so people can respond publicly.

CELEBRATING DIVERSITY
Unifying and Encouraging Individuality

31. Reach for the Stars

Purpose

Students will quickly learn the importance of giving 100%. Thank you to master educator **Paul Gulsvig** for this enlightening exercise.

Directions

1. Ask students to stretch as high as they can as if reaching for the stars. After the students do this, ask them again to stretch higher (which they will). Ask two more times for them to reach even higher. Most of them may grunt and groan a bit, but will be able to stretch each time you ask.

2. The students achieved more the second time, the third and even the fourth time.

3. Discuss with the class how that could even be possible? Your first instruction was to reach for the stars and as high as they could reach. If you asked them to do their best the very first time, how come they didn't give 100% the very first time? Were students not being honest the first time? Did they not know their potential? After finishing the exercise, discuss with the class about setting goals and how important it is to aim for the stars. Never settle.

Variations

Have students stretch jazz hands, speed walk from one place to another (timing them with a stopwatch) or throw a paper airplane as far as you can. Other activities could be to jump as high as you can, hold your breath as long as possible, or to keep eyes open without blinking for a period of time. Repeat the activity two or three times for the same results as above.

Tech Tips

So often, we are all capable of much more than is expected of us. Sometimes visual representations of goals and expectations help achieve a lofty goal. Try charting progress toward a goal. Download a goal chart and set your expectations high. Ask students to blog about progress and group assess how you can better support each other.

32. Divide and Unify!

Purpose

This is a fun and interactive game that reminds students of the similarities and differences between us. We are all unique and yet we all put our pants on one leg at a time. Even though we might go about it in different ways, the results are still the same. Let's celebrate diversity!

Directions

These "get-to-know-you-better" activities are fun and you'll be reminded others may approach things differently, but you can agree to disagree while working for the same goal. Ask your students to do the following:

- When stepping into a favorite pair of jeans, do you put your right or left leg in first?
- When folding arms across your chest, is your right arm on top or left?
- Clasp your hands together as in prayer. Is your right or left thumb on top when you clasp?
- If you are flirting and want to wink at someone, would you use your right or left eye?
- Which side of the bed do you tend to sleep on, or do you toss and turn?
- Sit down and cross your legs. Which leg do you use to cross over on top?
- Can you roll your tongue? (Yes or no?) Demonstrate.
- Can you roll your "rrrrr's"? (Yes or no?) Demonstrate.
- When eating ice cream, do you twirl or lick up and down?
- Do you prefer warm weather or cold?
- Do you roll or scrunch? (Toilet paper)
- If asked for a "thumbs up" sign, do you use your right or left thumb?
- Do you put your right or left contact in first? Do you have contacts/glasses or nothing?
- Do you eat one thing at a time on your plate or mix your food?
- When raising your hand, do you automatically raise your right or left hand first?
- Can you touch your toes with your fingers flat on the floor?
- Do you clap with your right hand on top or your left hand?
- Can you touch the tip of your tongue to your nose?
- Which shoe do you put on first – right or left?

Variations

1 + 1? Which ONE is better? Instead of giving students two choices, let the students come up with two favorites (category given by teacher). The class votes by show of hands which is better, this one or that one?

Tech Tips

You could make this an at-home or online writing assignment as well. An online discussion forum makes it easy to post questions and get students communicating outside of class.

33. Improv AND Improve

Purpose

This valuable IceBreaker game saves time, budget and brainstorming for the director. Students will feel ownership as they get to improv AND improve!

Directions

1. Break students into small groups. Students are given five minutes to improv and improve a situation or a perceived problem.

2. Students may ask for more explanation or clarification, but they need to analyze the situation – the analytical part of the assignment – and find a solution. The instructor provides the scenario and students work to problem-solve.

Ideas to Improv and Improve:

- Better standing or seating arrangement
- Use of cellphones in class
- Gum policy in class
- Extra storage
- Class safety
- Fundraising
- Talking in class
- Auditioning for solos and chairs
- Keeping focus in rehearsals
- Retreats
- Ticket sales
- Thanking patrons
- Learning music more rapidly
- Decorating the space

Variations

Body Language Speaks: We speak volumes with our bodies and our facial expressions. Demonstrate each move and ask students to determine what the body language or facial expressions are expressing.

- Folded arms – can't make me learn
- Shifting eyes or feet – need to focus to learn
- Arms to the side – I'm willing to learn
- Behind back – I can't wait to learn
- Body open – excited to be here; best position and ready to learn
- Eyebrows lifted (one or both) – questioning or excited to learn

Tech Tips

A record keeper could track which questions have been asked and the solutions. Put them on a projector so people can think through results and avoid asking the same question over and over.

34. Garbage In, Garbage Out

Purpose

If students are surrounded with garbage in what they see and hear (i.e. ugliness in society, trash talk and emotional rubbish), garbage will come out of their mouths. Be the person that takes out the garbage!

Directions

1. Each person grabs a piece of recycled paper to write on. If paper not available, this exercise will work as they symbolize the word in their head.

2. On recycled paper (or in their mind), request each student write one word on recycled paper stating something hurtful or negative that was said to them. Inform students that this information is private and will NOT be shared with anyone.

3. After writing the one-word piece of "garbage," physically crumple the paper and rip it into smaller pieces.

4. Each person will take a turn and toss their garbage into a garbage can. If no paper, they should go through the actions of tearing something and rub hands together as if getting rid of the paper.

5. Ask students if they feel comfortable sharing about a time that a teacher or another student made them feel good – the opposite of garbage.

Variations

Blazing Debris: If you sponsor students in a retreat setting, you can toss the shredded comments into a bonfire or a marked off area representing a bonfire. It is important for students to know that if you allow negative people in your life, negativity will follow in positively every area! Do not make comments that litter someone else's life. Stay positive and pay it forward. How can these affirming actions replace the debris?

Campus Cleanup: Our Butler Concert Choir takes at least one day a semester to go outside and clean up the campus. When 120 students walk around campus for 90 minutes picking up trash, it makes a huge difference. Take a photo and put on social media showing all the pounds of trash the Fine Arts students cleaned up for your administrators!

Tech Tips

Some students are more likely to be honest if they are anonymous. Use a discussion board or quiz environment and share responses with the group. Set up an anonymous quiz online using a site like Typeform.com so even you don't know who has submitted the information. This allows you to moderate a meaningful group discussion without anyone feeling like they are too scared to share.

35. It's SHOE Business

Purpose

This game provides a chance for students to be creative and let their imaginations "run" wild – all because of a pair of shoes!

Directions

1. Ask participating students to either a) bring a pair of shoes from home, or b) take off their shoes and set them along one of the walls in the rehearsal hall or the classroom.

2. The first person walks up to the shoes and stands behind a pair of shoes. They try to guess who belongs to the pair of shoes. Define and describe the personality of the person and what activities you think they do.

3. After describing the person, the student makes the final guess. If they guessed correctly, that person will step up and stand behind a pair of shoes and back to business.

Potential Shoe/Personality Questions

- Football or golf cleats?
- Runner or sprinter (which part of the sole is more worn)?
- New or heavily worn?
- Dance shoes?
- Outdoor shoes?
- Dress shoes?
- Team shoes (dance team, cheerleading, athletic)?
- Sandals (need feet to breathe)?
- Comfy shoes?
- Artistic originals (initials, colors and markings)?

Variations

Shoe Grab: Take ONE shoe off and keep one shoe on. Throw the shoe you took off into a large pile in the center of the room. When given the OK, randomly grab another shoe. The goal is to find the person who belongs to the shoe you are holding. Try to stand behind the person that matches your find. It will create a fun twisting shape. The day we tried this in class, everyone was wearing black jazz shoes. It gave us lots to laugh about for the rest of the year!

Tech Tips

Try this technique with online usernames. Have students write their usernames and put the papers in a bowl. Select usernames from the bowl and guess who they belong to! It is fun to see what people have come up with, and most students' usernames are not their actual name and provide insight into their values and personality.

36. Bucket Listing

Purpose

This activity encourages students to dream and dream big. It is a proven fact that if goals are written down, these goals are much more likely to be reached. Ask teachers to participate in this activity. We ALL need to dream big!

Directions

1. A **bucket list** is a dream list that covers events and activities that a person is interested in doing before they "kick the bucket." Some popular bucket lists include: skydiving, solving a Rubik's® Cube, going on a dog sled expedition, eating Belgian waffles in Belgium, visiting all the major league baseball stadiums, flying in a hot air balloon, swimming with dolphins, crossing the intersection at Abbey Road, learning how to skateboard, performing on Broadway, riding an elephant, falling in love and writing an IceBreaker book!

2. Create the perfect bucket list for yourself.

3. Then, work as a team and design a bucket list for a smaller subgroup (clarinet section, tenors, stage crew, percussionists).

4. Create a bucket list for your school. Do it as a game, but the results might be helpful to administration and others.

Variations

Bucket Quest: Why is a bucket list important to have? What types of things are on other people's bucket lists? When do you expect to have crossed everything off? Will you?

Bucket of Chicken: Devise one item from a bucket list to accomplish in a week's time. Prove you didn't chicken out of the activity by posting a snapchat of the individual(s) accomplishing the goal. Be brave and don't chicken out!

Time Bucket: Write goals in a sealed time capsule. Get permission to put the capsule in a school vault, music library or bury outside. Be sure to create a reminder of the date to open. This could include future dreams and a photo of the class. Do this for each incoming class and have a celebration on the final day when it is time to open the "Time Bucket".

Tech Tips

A simple list app, such as Google Keep, is great for bucket listing. You can create collaborative lists where groups of users can add and check off items. Try creating a "bucket list" for your whole ensemble and see how many you can check off together!

37. Real or REALLY?!?!

Purpose

Get to know each other by hearing several true tales about each person. Watch facial and body language to determine when people are telling a "tall tale." This turns into a great time to work on storytelling and speaking in public.

Directions

1. Take turns talking about yourself and telling outrageous – but true – stories. Each person is given 60 seconds to speak quickly and give as many facts about yourself as you can.

2. However, one of the facts will be fictional. If a listening student feels that fact is not true, they raise both hands in shrug and say "*REALLY?!?!*"

   • I can play five musical instruments.

   • I have been to six countries in the past year.

   • My best friend was Miss Kansas (or whatever state you are from).

   • I have eaten octopus.

   • I have received more than 20 speeding tickets.

   • I love the smell of skunk.

   • I was recruited to play on the chess team.

   • My dog flunked obedience school.

   • I have watched *Sound of Music* ten times.

   • I built a 3D printer.

   • I can touch my tongue to my nose.

   • I met Jimmy Fallon.

Variations

Speak Fast and Furious: Teacher chooses a subject (i.e. cooking, cheerleaders, chocolate, laundry, computers, cell phone manners, coffee, swimsuit shopping, cutest movie star, vacations, trees, shampoo, or favorite teacher). Students partner up, then one student has to speak as fast as possible for two solid minutes about that subject. No gathering thoughts or stopping speech allowed. Students need to commit! This is when creativity begins. Students should switch partners and a new topic is given.

Tech Tips

Add to the silliness with a classic game show buzzer sound. You can find many online, or use a free app such as The Ultimate Buzzer. Have students buzz in with silly sound effects when they suspect someone is telling their tall tale.

38. You're Kidding?

Purpose

Sometimes we get too serious and stress about the small stuff! It is time to remember your childhood days. For some of the participants, it may not be that long ago. Whatever the age or experience, you will enjoy thinking back on your childhood. All participants will make connections with this exercise.

Directions

Think back to the youngest age you remember and answer the following.

- First holiday you remember celebrating and how?
- First pet and the pet's name?
- First big trip and where did you go?
- First time you rode a bike? Could you stop?
- First time in the hospital (hospitalized or just visiting)?
- First broken bone? What was it and how did you break it?
- First time you were embarrassed?
- First time you lost someone important?
- First day of school?
- First time you helped in the kitchen?
- First present you purchased? What was the gift?
- First time you were really scared?
- First storm you remember?
- First sleepover?
- First time you got in big trouble? Why?!?
- First musical experience that changed your life?
- First time you knew what you wanted to do when you grew up?

Variations

Scar Stories: Students sit in a circle. Ask for volunteers to share (and show) a "scar story". Each volunteer explains when and how they got the scar. Remind students to keep it PG when sharing – AND showing. This will be one of the student's favorite IceBreaker questions. No kidding!

Tech Tips

Encourage students to start using an app like Timehop with their photos and social profiles. Timehop reminds students of what they were doing on any day in the past. Every time a photo of a retreat, concert, or activity shows back up, they will think of being a part of your class and be more likely to positively contribute to your program in the future.

39. Living Statue

Purpose

This exercise offers class members the opportunity to physically shape and mold a group of students into a statue representing the past, the present and finally visualizing the future. Build memories and use personal experiences to make this happen. Ask for volunteers, as this will not be something everyone will feel comfortable sharing. Beware: this seemingly simple exercise can be a far-reaching emotional game. Do your expectations help or hinder the reactions?

Directions

1. The "artist" must position the statue in a pose that demonstrates how he or she perceives contributions from each of his or her family members. Create your "family" using fellow students in the class. "Family" might consist of people at home or it might mean the friends you have made and the people that believe in you that are right there in the classroom.

2. Students will make three statues with the same people in each "living statue".

3. Do the expectations we place on our family members hinder or help them?

   - Past statue: the artist will choose an important memory.
   - Present: something current and what is most relevant in your life right now!
   - Future: how you envision your family in the future.

Variations

Debrief by talking through this exercise. Did you like the artist trying to change you? What were some of your frustrations? How could this exercise be more effective?

Pick one thing you would like to see in the group and choose to model that in your own life. The only person you can truly change is yourself. It would be nice to have an artist present at all times, but we know that is not possible. But … if it was possible, what would you want them to sculpt around you?

Tech Tips

Some students might have some delightfully awkward family photos. Try recreating them and sharing them online with the original members, or you can simply take photos of each living statue to save as keepsakes.

40. Sushi Shuffle

Purpose

Once your class starts getting to know each other, use this game designed to help individuals know more about each other's likes, dislikes, personalities and leadership styles.

Directions

1. Communicate to the students that they must form a line in the order of who loves sushi the very most to those who hate sushi the most. If group is large, split into two or more lines with 12-20 participants in each line.

2. Don't give any other instructions. Students must work as a team to determine the order of the line by figuring out the degree of liking or disliking of sushi and where to stand in the line.

3. Someone may say "I haven't tried sushi" or "I don't know what sushi is," so how do I fit into the line? Refrain from answering and allow the students to figure out a solution. There isn't necessarily a right or wrong order. Most importantly, students must learn to accept all members and figure out how to work as a team. There are degrees of acceptance and understanding – and perhaps not everyone fits in the line every time. Even so, students have to learn to come together, especially when it seems there are no rules and no organization.

Variations

The list of possible topics is endless. Choose something polarizing for discussion or silly to get people feeling positive. Here are some ideas:

- Choose a different unusual food.
- Compare vacation destinations.
- How much did you like/dislike a popular movie?
- Country Music is the greatest. Agree or disagree?
- Fan of a sporting team or not a fan?
- Play a song and have students rate it.

This or That: If your group has a hard time shuffling in line, start with some simple comparison questions to get them used to running back and forth and progress to the Sushi Shuffle. Players must choose their preference and the faster you shout out questions, the more shuffling they will have to do!

Tech Tips

If you need some really wacky and sometimes very challenging questions to answer, search a website like either.io. You can enter topics and see questions other people have submitted! Many of these may not be appropriate for all audiences, so plan your questions ahead of time!

41. X = X

Purpose

The **X = X** equation is as simple as it sounds. Whatever emotion the student feels on stage is exactly what emotion each audience member will feel. It works in life as well. If you are apathetic, people will act that way around you. If you are excited to be there, people will pick up that vibe and reflect. Thank you **David Connolly** for sharing your wisdom so many years ago. This concept has been used in our classrooms ever since we had the privilege of learning this lesson from the master teacher.

Directions

1. Choose one of the songs you are studying or about to perform.
2. Ask one student to read the lyrics of the song. If an instrumental selection, read the story about the piece or composer notes.
3. Discuss as a class what the lyrics or story is saying and then have students give suggestions of emotions they feel best represents the song overall.
4. Discuss the emotions and continue to whittle away until the group has decided on one emotion.
5. Repeat for each and every number you are studying and/or performing. The goal is to establish a different emotion for each song. For example, if the ensemble is performing seven songs, there should be seven various emotions that are represented.

Variations

Make a poster that includes the show order with the song emotion for each song and hang it in the classroom so students are reminded daily of what emotion they are trying to feel throughout the rehearsal. **X = X**. If accomplished, the songs will have their own personality and will relate better to audiences.

Turn **X = X** into a quiz, to see if performers remember the discussion about the song lyrics and the one-word emotion.

Post the information on the class web page to remind students of the goal (and show order).

Physically remind yourself that **X = X** by making an X with your forearms. Bring elbows up to form an equal sign and then tilt the elbows back down to repeat the X symbol.

Tech Tips

Improve the ability to represent emotion by having students sing the same song with contrary emotions. Video or audio record the performances and invite students to assess which is most effective and which parts do not yet fully realize the emotional intent.

42. Step Up and Say YES!

Purpose

This IceBreaker explores the common interests and connections shared by members of the class.

Directions

Form a circle and take one step forward each time the answer is "yes." If the answer is "no" or you aren't sure, take one step back. The goal is not getting to the center of the circle, but getting to know common and interesting facts about each other.

Potential Questions

- Are you involved with music 3 or more days a week?
- Did you eat breakfast this morning?
- Were you on time this morning?
- Did you have quiet time (yoga, devotional, reading, prayer, eyes shut)?
- Have you exercised this week?
- Have you stopped at a fast food place more than once a day?
- Do you play 3 or more instruments? Proficiently?
- Do you know everyone's name in the circle? Last names? Middle names?
- Did you do anything nice for anyone today? This week? This year?
- Have you driven over the speed limit this week? (If answer is yes, step back!)
- Have you traveled overseas?
- Have you eaten a home cooked meal this week?
- Have you prepared a home cooked meal this week?
- Have you read a book in the past week?
- Did you make your bed before you left this morning?
- Are you glad you are here?

The authors are so glad you are trying this game and getting to know each other so EVERYONE take 5 big steps forward and group hug! Celebrate the steps you took and remember we are all on different journeys. No one is walking in your shoes, and you are not walking in theirs!

Variations

Chair-breakers: Check out *IceBreakers 1*, page 30. If you need more questions, contact the authors.

Tech Tips

For an online or in-person class that is highly connected, try putting these polls into an assessment tool such as polleverywhere.com or tophat.com. You can get real-time graphs on the responses, and students can respond via text, email or twitter!

PROBLEM SOLVING
Turning Stressful Conditions into Working Conditions

43. Phantom of the Classroom

Purpose

Use your deduction skills to figure out who is the "Phantom" before the "Phantom" finds you!

Directions

1. Teacher secretly selects one student to star as the Phantom.

2. Students mingle around the room, shaking hands with each other and looking into each other's eyes.

3. The Phantom shakes hands and winks. IF a student gets winked at, she has 10 seconds to sing her way to the floor – making a slow opera death (gasping, clutching heart, weeping, grabbing head, etc.)

4. The goal is to guess who the Phantom is before he winks at you. If a student wants to guess, she stops the game and announces her suspicion to the whole group. If correct, she is the winner and is applauded. If not, she must immediately stage her own dramatic death, and the game continues until the Phantom is found.

5. The teacher will select a different Phantom each game.

Variations

Survival: Divide the class into smaller groups. Explain there was a shipwreck and imagine the students in the group landed on a deserted island. They need to find 10 items on the island to survive. Name those items and rank in the order of importance. Compare each group's answers. Compare the answers with the teacher. Problem solved and you survived!

Tech Tips

Students really get into their operatic demise. Most smart phones can record slow motion videos. Combine a few slow-motion videos with an app like Magisto, which creates compilation videos, and you've got a show-stopping silly video!

44. Human Instruments

Purpose

This game provides an outlet for students to work together, to think "out of the box" and to be connected physically.

Directions

1. Divide students into groups of seven or eight people.

2. Ask students to build a type of apparatus that does something related to Fine Arts. Each project should include design and purpose. The *"human instrument"* must include every person in the group AND students must be physically connected – no one can stand alone. Give a time limit and a reminder that all need to be involved in the process.

Ideas for the Human Instrument

- New type of musical instrument
- Ticket taker
- Program folder
- Instrument that measures volume
- Machine that sets up the stage
- Machine that tears down the stage
- Video recorder that edits
- Folder cabinet that supplies pencils
- Cell phone silencer for audience members
- Machine that adds applause sound effects during performances
- Role-taking device
- Snack maker for performers back stage
- Apparatus that cleans and repairs instruments

Variations

After the "instrument" demonstrates its purpose, require each group to change the function and improve upon the design. After the exercise, discuss how it felt when asked to improve or change the instrument? Did individuals work harder or give up because they were frustrated in being asked to change the product?

Tech Tips

Groups of people in public places doing ridiculous things create viral marketing gems. Try taking your Human Instrument game to the mall or a movie theatre with your students and get as many people to join in as possible! Post it online as a fun flash mob from your choir to promote an upcoming event or fundraiser. You'd be shocked how many people are willing to join in with the game if you announce you are looking for players.

45. To Be or Not To ...

Purpose

Students are assigned the dreaded assignment - write a Haiku poem. This will not be such a dreaded assignment when done with classmates who have been given an endearing topic. Double bonus - winning Haikus could be shared on social media, in a program book or for advertising.

Directions

1. The instructor will divide students into groups of three. Students can write this down or each one of the three can memorize a line.

2. Give the assignment to write a Haiku poem (short form of Japanese poetry written with three lines, the first and third have five syllables and the middle line has seven syllables). Instructor will provide the topic.

   Suggested Poetry Topics
   - Rehearsal etiquette
   - Specific song title
   - First time on stage
   - Teacher's pet peeves
   - Costume malfunctions
   - Marching Band shows
   - Orchestra members sitting in the pit for musicals
   - Fundraisers
   - Supporting the Fine Arts
   - Early morning rehearsals
   - Music theory
   - Music contest
   - Future of the Arts
   - The Last Show

Variations

Poetic Types: Write a poem in another form to share. Use Free Verse, Cinquain (5 line poem), Epic poem (long!), Name Poem (acronyms), Sonnets (Shakespeare-ish) or a Christmas Carol (change the words). Invite the English faculty to make a cross-departmental assignment. Win-win for everyone involved!

Tech Tips

Most Haikus created will be less than 140 characters, which is the perfect length for your Twitter channel! If your group doesn't have a Twitter handle, these haikus could be your perfect first tweet. Create poems about the group, concerts, etc. and use them to entertain followers!

46. Villain or Hero?

Purpose

Students get a chance to be as melodramatic as possible with this interactive IceBreaker. Some will put their acting skills to good use, while others are participating by booing the villain, cheering for the hero and sighing for the heroine. The audience calls the shots this time.

Directions

1. Ask three students to step out of the room so the rest of the class can choose a scene for the actors to perform. The scene will be very simple.

2. The twist is that the actors have no idea what they will be asked to do. They do know they will do something typically performed in a Melodrama and they know which of the three parts they will be playing.

3. The three students play the part of the dainty heroine, the stalwart hero and dastardly villain. The class will use booing and applause to encourage or discourage the three actors. If the heroine and hero are supposed to be hugging, the class will cheer as the two of them get closer, and boo and hiss as they step away from each other. The class cheers will guide the actors into doing the "right" thing. A standing ovation is achieved when the actors finish the scene.

Ideas for Melodramatic Scenes
(Let the actors know who will be starring in the scenes below.)

- Hero and Heroine hug
- Heroine passes out in Villain's arms
- Villain and Hero freeze in fake fight scene
- Hero and Villain end back to back
- All three are hugging
- The Hero has one foot on the Villain's back as Villain is passed out on the floor
- Heroine jumps in the Hero's arms
- Heroine tied to the railroad tracks by the Villain
- The Villain puts the Heroine over his shoulder
- Heroine curtseys and the Villain and Hero bow

Variations

The instructor has the option of teaching about the modern-day Melodrama, the stock characters and the intermission Oleo acts. Perform your own version for younger grades.

Tech Tips

If you have a projector cart available, try projecting a large picture of a scene to help students get into character. We've moved risers to create a "stage" up next to the projection screen so students can act out their melodrama with a digital full set!

47. Connecting Phrases

Purpose

This game is a sneaky way to encourage students to sing independently. It will also help broaden the students' horizons in the world of music and lyrics. If the instructor is able, take notes, as some of their suggestions could turn into great suggestions for future literature.

Directions

1. This game can be done in small groups or students can compete individually.

2. The instructor begins the game by singing one line of a famous song. Whatever word or phrase is at the end of this phrase must be used to start the new song.

3. Each team has 15 seconds to come up with a song. If the team can't come up with lyrics that match up, the other team gets a point.

4. Connect phrases until students lose interest. It is lots of fun and students will like competing on teams. Use this activity as a reward for good behavior.

   Connecting Phrase Examples

   - A hunting we will go, A Hunting we will go… high ho the merry o, a hunting we will GO
   - GO tell it on the mountain, Over the hills and everywhere, Go, tell it on the MOUNTAIN…
   - Coming round the MOUNTAIN when she comes, she'll be coming round the mountain when she COMES…
   - COME on and hear, Come on and hear… It's the best band in the LAND
   - LAND of the pilgrims' pride, From ev'ry mountainside, Let freedom RING!
   - RING around the rosy, pocketful of posies…

   Now it's your turn to continue the game.

Variations

Compound It! This is the same idea but works for younger students. It doesn't have a musical element but will get them ready for "Connecting Phrases" game (i.e. hot dog, dog dish, dish towel, towel rack, etc.)

Tech Tips

Record the musical volley and see if you can create a great mix-tape version of the song! You can edit out all the talking and laughing using free software like Audacity. Then take it to the next level by adding a percussion track, created in an app like GarageBand!

48. Musical Lingo Bingo

Purpose

This is a physical activity that also increases the musical vocabulary.

Directions

1. Instruct students to stand around the perimeters of the room.

2. Inform students you will provide a musical word or phrase. If they demonstrate, define or answer correctly, they will run to a spot in the room, elbows ready to link with another student.

3. Say a word from the list below.

4. Those students who know the definition run to the center of the room and try to link up elbows with others. Once five people are linked, the students all must yell simultaneously "Lingo Bingo!"

5. As in the game Bingo, the teacher will check to make sure the group won fair and square. The teacher will ask each one or more persons to answer or prove their knowledge.

Musical Lingo Bingo Suggestions

- Euphonium
- Obbligato
- Affettuoso
- Countertenor
- Passing tone
- Tarantella
- Velocissimo
- Tutti
- Rubato
- Antiphonal
- Broken chord
- Scat
- Requiem

Variations

See the following page for a list of statements for "Musical Lingo Bingo."

Tech Tips

If your class is less mobile, or you need a Bingo activity that uses classic sheets, there are SO MANY free online sites to create Bingo cards. We use bingobaker.com because you can create a playable online game that works with iPads, or an easy-to-print PDF of multiple cards in a variety of sizes.

Statements for Musical Lingo Bingo

- I can sing or play the "Star Spangled Banner."
- I can play a brass instrument.
- I am currently taking piano lessons.
- I know the difference between major and minor keys.
- I sing in my church choir or play in a community band each week.
- I know the difference between melody and harmony.
- I know what a concertmaster does.
- I can play a string instrument.
- I can read bass clef.
- I know what instrument is used to tune an orchestra.
- I know the difference between a band and an orchestra.
- I can play chopsticks on the piano.
- I can tune a guitar.
- I know a folk song.
- I have seen a musical performance.
- I know the difference between hearing music and listening to music.
- I went to a musical performance in the last month.
- I know the difference between "classical" and "pop" music.
- I listen to music even when I am not in class or in a vehicle.
- I know where there is a music store in the vicinity.
- I use music to relax.
- I could write music down so another person could perform it.
- I can name three well-known composers.
- I see a connection between aural and visual art.
- I can play/sing by ear.
- I have more than 2,000 songs on my playlist.
- I can name 3 singers from the past who have influenced the music of today.
- I can spell "soprano."
- I know what SATB stands for.
- I know what "pizzicato" means.
- I have read a book or seen a movie about a composer.
- I can sing the school fight song.
- I can tell you the most prolific movie composer.
- In the future, I would insist my child play in the band or take piano lesson.

49. Clap 'n Slap

Purpose

Watch and then demonstrate a choreographed pattern. Can you repeat the pattern? Instead of having someone tell you what to do, use your brain and turn it into a game.

Directions

1. Demonstrate the pattern below and see if students can learn by watching. Normally students are told what to do. Watch, listen and figure out the patterns involved.

2. Can you repeat the pattern with a partner? Once you figure it out, how fast can you go? Turbo time!

Face partner. Clap in front of your chest and open both hands and put in front of your chest, palms facing out to slap partner's hands. The pattern is:

1 clap and **1 slap** partner

1 clap and **2 slaps** partner

1 clap and **3 slaps** partner

1 clap and **4 slaps** partner

1 clap and **3 slaps** partner

1 clap and **2 slaps** partner

1 clap and **1 slap** partner

2 claps and 1 slap partner

3 claps and 1 slap partner

4 claps and 1 slap partner

3 claps and 1 slap partner

2 claps and 1 slap partner

1 clap and 1 slap partner

Start all over again.

Variations

Circle Clap 'n Slap: Once the game is achieved with a partner, try the game sitting in a circle. Clap 'n slap partner by crossing hands and touching hands with people sitting next to you.

Create Clap 'n Slap: Ask students to create clap 'n slap patterns. Of course, the student must memorize and be able to repeat the pattern in order to teach their creation.

Tech Tips

Advanced students might need a little pressure to clap 'n slap, so try using a metronome! Free apps are all around, like ProMetronome. A faster tempo may mean more mistakes. If you have a bigger ensemble, a metronome can speed up this game.

50. Chartbusters

Purpose

Students use their "inner mind" to achieve the answer. This activity is a variation on the old standard "Name That Tune." In this game, the students will utilize solfège or Kodaly hand symbols. "Chartbusters" uses problem solving skills and is a great way to begin each and every rehearsal.

Directions

1. The director should have several songs in mind. If solfège doesn't come naturally, have the first line of the tune written out beforehand. Some ideas for simple tunes: Jingle Bells, Three Blind Mice, Joy to the World, the Alphabet song, Are You Sleeping? Skip to My Lou, etc.

2. The instructor asks the class to watch her hand symbols. Students will internalize the pitches inside their head and shouldn't hum along.

3. Students raise hands as they figure out the name of the song.

4. The instructor keeps repeating until several students recognize the tune.

5. If they guess correctly, they score a point for their section (woodwinds, percussion, tenors, etc.).

Variations

Call and Response: Instead of answering with the name of the tune, the student can solfège the rest of the phrase. For instance, if the teacher demonstrates, "Twinkle, twinkle, little star", the student can respond with the next line, "How I wonder what you are" with solfège.

Clap Response: Add the element of rhythm. Use directions above, but clap the rhythm of the selected song instead of adding the melody component.

I Can Solfège That Tune, Can You? Place students in small groups and see which group can figure out the tune. To make this a little less difficult, make categories and let the groups choose a musical category (i.e. holiday selections, nursery rhymes, patriotic tunes, classic rock, famous Classical tunes, etc.).

Tech Tips

Translate a catchy part of a Billboard top chart to solfège and **project the solfège** on the wall for the students. Students attempt to figure it out without making a sound. If it takes too long, tell them the artist. This challenges their ability to think intervallically.

51. Taking Musical Shape

Purpose

Several concepts are combined in this fun IceBreaker game such as listening skills, moving to a beat, teamwork, creativity and thinking outside the box. This game is about to take (a musical) shape!

Directions

1. Students are divided into teams. Play music and the students move individually around the room, keeping time to the music – walking to the beat. Add clapping on 2 and 4 or on the "and's" of the steady beat, if you want to really make this more challenging and take it up a notch.

2. When the music stops, the teacher says, I'm looking for a _____ shape.

3. The members of the team assemble together and position themselves in such a manner that the arrangement of the entire team forms that symbol. Once the teams have all accomplished the shape of the musical element, time the activity and move on. See how fast the team can work to accomplish the completion of the shape.

Ideas for Musical Shapes

- Treble clef
- Bass clef
- Quarter rest
- Repeat sign
- Dotted half note
- Crescendo
- Decrescendo

- Phrase
- Sharp
- Flat
- Natural sign
- Fermata
- Star
- Free for all (Group chooses their own musical shape)

Variations

Extension Magic: Do the same activity but use an extension cord to help create the shape. Use the list above or ask students to create their own shapes.

Silent Extension Magic? A real test in silent communication!

Tech Tips

Load a list into a random name picker online (such as www.miniwebtool.com/random-name-picker) so your choices are as unpredictable as possible. The longer the list of shapes, the less likely you are to repeat.

SUPPORT AND APPRECIATE

2, 4, 6, 8 Who do we appreciate!?

52. BirthRIGHT?

Purpose

Students can commiserate with each other about their birth order. They are given a chance to quickly connect over shared experiences. Right or wrong, there is scientific evidence that the order of your birth and parenting skills define behavior.

Directions

1. Students divide themselves into four corners of the room, depending on these four groups: youngest child, middle child, oldest child and only child.

2. Give students a chance to discuss the following: What do you have in common with the others in your corner and are there pros and cons of birth order? Are the assumptions about birth order personalities accurate?

3. How do firstborns get along with other firstborns? Firstborns and the baby of the family? Only children and middle children? Can you think of relationships that speak to these facts? Do they follow the trend? Is it your Birth RIGHT?

Birth Order Stereotypes

- Firstborn tends to be the leader of the pack, reliable, conscientious, controlling, an over achiever, responsible

- Middle Child often feels left out, is a people-pleaser, has large social circles, is a peacemaker, rebellious, and fairness-obsessed

- Youngest Child is often fun-loving, outgoing, self-centered, manipulative, uncomplicated, an attention-seeker, charming, a free spirit

- Only Child monopolizes attention, is mature, a perfectionist, conscientious, diligent and a leader

Variations

Best Personal Value: Ask a class to share personal values. What are the best values to possess? Is one value more important than other values? What makes us lose those values? (I.e. health, time, energy, society, family traits, tradition, education?) Is it helpful to understand where someone is coming from? Do we make excuses or emphasize?

Tech Tips

There is research under way regarding how birth order impacts online personality. Are there parallels regarding how groups interact online? What apps are favored and what online activities valued? Who participates less in the digital world? Personality discussions will always be interesting and force your groups to open up to each other.

53. Thank You Very Much

Purpose

Encouraging thankfulness is one of the best things a teacher can do and teaching students to say thank you is one of the best lessons a teacher can teach. This is one activity that will motivate students to think and appreciate not just those in front of the spotlight, but those behind the scenes as well.

Directions

1. Ask the ensemble to reflect on how different – and difficult – life would be without certain groups of people supporting and appreciating their work.

2. Make a mental list of all those that contribute to the program.

3. Openly discuss the value and importance of each of the people who support your classroom.

This is a great way for building up a program or a group of people. To prepare, the director should be able to give some examples.

Consider adding the following to your list:

Accompanist(s), choreographer, band, alto section, stage crew, parents, audience members, theatre techs, lighting person, sound person, PR people, fundraisers, principal, superintendent, alumni, the community, or anyone else you choose to mention.

What would happen if the director wasn't there? Would rehearsals continue or classes teach themselves? Find out this important information <u>before</u> having a substitute teacher sub for you.

Variations

Follow this IceBreaker with a letter writing activity for a win-win situation. Provide students with paper and envelopes to write a hand-written thank you letter to the people who help support your program. We also regularly ask students to think of a teacher who has inspired them and write a note of thanks.

Tech Tips

Consider sending a thank you postcard from the group. Take a photo of the group and use an app like Touchnote, or PhotoCard by Bill Atkinson, to send a postcard via good old-fashioned US Post. Guest clinicians, choreographers and audience members love to receive heartfelt thanks!

54. Building Up

Purpose

Try this exercise to build or repair relationships in the room. It takes a long time to rebuild a family atmosphere. It's easier if you don't tear down people in the first place. Celebrate them instead of judge them. You aren't walking in their shoes. Talk the talk AND walk the walk. The foundation of the building begins with the leadership team. Build from the groundwork and make sure your infrastructure is solid.

Directions

1. Once a week, invite a few students, staff or faculty members to secretly find other students in the classroom that have had a rough week or are going through tough times.

2. Ask "builder" students to say hello, smile or secretly share a positive comment. This is not a secret buddy exercise, as it will remain confidential. This game won't be advertised or discussed in class.

3. Make your classroom a positive environment and one that students rush to be in. The more secretive the better and in fact, the teacher will never mention this in class and should communicate with the "builders" privately.

Variations

First Week of Building: Pair older builders with younger ones the first week of class. Have older builders deliver a handwritten note in a folder, a small piece of candy on their chair, a bottle of water, or even a smile and head nod. A simple act of caring can change lives.

Fine Arts folks need to be more proactive about retention and work to keep numbers in our programs. More importantly, this is the kind of simple and caring thing a teacher can do. Implementing this activity helps students realize the power of a positive word. Teaching students to be compassionate and caring may be more important than anything else you teach all year.

Statistics prove it is easier and more cost effective to retain students rather than recruiting new students. Take care and build up those students you do have. Those students will go out and be great recruiters for your program. This is how you can truly build and grow your program – starting from a solid foundation.

Tech Tips

Try communicating with students by sending a positive message through text. Let them know you are thinking of them and believing in them. If you don't feel comfortable giving your phone number, use a service like Remind.com to send free messages to any cell phone. Students respond much better to personal messages than email or generic Facebook posts.

55. Acronym Yourself

Purpose

This project gives students a chance to reinforce classmates' names while thinking of positive attributes for each person. The instructor will also benefit from participating in this IceBreaker activity. Don't be shy. Acronym yourself.

Directions

Using the school ensemble name for the acronym, ask all the ensemble members to think of words that describe individuals' hobbies, talents, skills or interests to carry out this project.

Students can work as one unit, in smaller teams or individually. Use words that interest or define the person. This can be shared out loud, or students can write the information down.

The only rule when composing? Only positive and affirming words are allowed when you acronym yourself.

M = Manilow fan
A = Amazon Prime member
C = Creative
K = Kansas

U = Unique
D = Dog lover
L = Lucy's dad
A = Adventuresome
N = Nonjudgmental
D = Digitally-Minded

Variations

The wordplay could also be used with a person's last name, middle name, instrument played, desired career, favorite soft drink, favorite movie, favorite band, sport played, team, favorite holiday. The list is never-ending.

UN-cross Word Puzzle: Why UN-cross? Only use positive words in the un-cross word puzzle. No negative or "cross" words are allowed. Use names to create the un-cross word puzzle.

Tech Tips

If you need help coming up with acronyms there are plenty of online tools with word banks. As an example, try www.nameacronym.net, where the default acronym search only returns positive words!

56. Not I …

Purpose

In our world today, conversations are filled with talk about ego and self. We live in a self-centered society and need to be reminded not to get so absorbed in ourselves and our problems. This short exercise reminds us to think of others and not dwell on ourselves. This exercise works great to help students learn to connect and appreciate each other.

Directions

1. Pair students up with a partner. The younger partner speaks first and the older person listens.

2. Speak with your partner for two minutes about something very important to you BUT you cannot use the word "I" or "me". Talk as fast as you can. The other person must remain silent. There should be no pauses in the conversation. Then reverse the roles.

3. How difficult was it to speak and not use these two pronouns? Which one of you had the hardest time with this exercise?

4. Try this exercise and talk about a time you made a mistake. This time you cannot use the word "but." ("It was my fault but…" won't fly.)

Variations

It's Me! Have the listener try to mimic the facial expressions and hand movements of the person speaking. The listener is never allowed to speak. Creating a clone makes both parties hyper aware of each other and communication skills – or lack of skills.

Unending Inquiries: How long can a group carry on a conversation answering only with questions? For example:
1st person: Wasn't that a great show?
2nd person: What wasn't to love?
3rd person: Was there a love song in the show?
4th person: Isn't every song somehow about love?
5th person: Aren't you a romantic?
6th person: Like you aren't?
This game works great on long bus rides. Right? What else would you be doing? Inquiring minds want to know!?

Tech Tips

Video the "It's Me!" variation and play it back for an assessment of how well you move and connect with each other. You could also encourage the conversation to be an entirely physical one with no talking and see how they mirror each other.

57. The NewlyFED Game

Purpose

Sometimes, the silliest facts help us all get to know each other. We can laugh together and even make fun of ourselves. You'll have fun adding questions to the list!

Directions

1. Select 3 girls and 3 guys to begin the game. After they choose partners, send the 3 girls to the hallway or another room that is soundproof so they can't hear the guys' answers.

2. Ask 3 guys to step to the front of the room and answer 3 questions. Each guy answers the question how he thinks the girl would answer. Write answers on their cell phones OR answer out loud.

3. Bring the 3 girls back, standing next to their partner. Ask the girls the same questions one at a time. After the first girl answers, the guy will share his answer and see if they match. If so, their team gets a point. The class is divided into three teams so they can cheer. When this round is done, it is the guys' turn to leave the room so the girls can answer new questions, trying to decide how their partner would answer the question.

4. Next round, 6 new people – 2 from each of the 3 teams.

Potential NewlyFed Questions

- If she says she wants one slice of pizza, will she really only eat one slice?
- Will she ask before she takes food off a friend's plate?
- Does she like quinoa? Eggplant? Tapioca? Gooseberry jam? Goat cheese? Endive?
- Does she like her campfire marshmallows completely burnt or lightly toasted?
- Would he eat a fried tarantula?
- How many tacos could he put down at one sitting?
- How spicy does he like his wings?
- Would he rather spend time playing a sport or eating donuts with the guys?
- What is Spirulina? Arugula? Rhubarb?
- What would his favorite State Fair food be?
- What is the weirdest thing you've eaten on a stick?
- What is your favorite Girl Scout cookie flavor?
- Do you drink milk from the carton?

Variations

The NewlyMET Game: New relationships? He said, she said.

The NewlySAID Game: Quotes from teachers. Were you listening?

The NewlyDEAD Game: Zombie-related questions! Thanks Zane! ;)

The NewlyREAD Game: Questions from an assigned reading. See who knows the material best.

The NewlyLEAD Game: Bring in various leaders from the school and the community. Can you read their minds to predict their vision with the leadership they intend to provide?

Tech Tips

Have each pairing take a photo as though they are a couple. Encourage them to act the part (NewlyFED: eating/feeding, NewlySAID: act like the teacher, NewlyDEAD: be the undead)! Use a quick file transfer service like Airplay to post the photos on a screen during the game.

58. Wishing Well

Purpose

Use this well-wishing game to shift the focus from the teacher to the students. A classroom is strongest when students feel valued and respected by each other. By sharing personal thoughts and anecdotes, students and teachers will create an environment that is diverse, inclusive and open for learning.

Directions

1. Divide the class in half and form two circles, one inside the other. This game works best with equal numbers; if you have an odd number make sure the instructor participates!

2. Play or sing a positive song while the two circles walk in opposite directions. One of our favorite songs to use in this exercise is Greg Gilpin's *Why We Sing*. This piece was written for the Butler Showchoir Camp, so it has a special place in our hearts and celebrates the meaning behind the music.

3. The instructor should randomly stop the music by raising his or her hand or turning off the recording.

4. Students immediately face their partner in the opposite circle and share one kind word about each other. Continue with the song and repeat the exercise until the positive vibes fill the room!

If you don't have a song or access to music, have everyone say a positive phrase and stop when it is over! Or, combine this game with "Zoom Around the Room" on page 14 to get people really moving and appreciating!

Variations

Flashbacks: Instead of a kind word, have participants share a kind memory of each other or a class activity.

Positive Presents: Have students explain why their "presence" is a present and important at this point in their life/year.

Wishful Thinking: A positive outlook or idea of a bright future can shape a student's reality. Have them share a well-wish for their partner's life or future.

Tech Tips

Like a secret pal, anonymous kind words can turn a day around. Have your students send you their favorite positive quotes or inspirational phrases. Share one each day or each week with the class. If you keep it completely anonymous, it creates a safe environment for sharing. Use Remind or a messaging platform built into your curriculum to share with everyone. This may be the only positive or kind words a student hears today.

59. And the Award Goes to...

Purpose

This game gives a tremendous boost of affirmative words to those behind the scenes. It is a tangible reminder that we need and appreciate those who are supporting and cheering us on. Imagine doing everything without helpers. We'd rather not!

Directions

1. Divide class into smaller groups of 4-5 people. Be sure one imaginative person is in each of the smaller groups.

2. Give each small group access to a piece of paper and a pen, marker board or sidewalk chalk.

3. Design an award for various individuals and groups that support your program or class throughout the year. Be careful to think this through, as you want to be very careful no one is left off the list.

4. Instead of putting in the program or recognizing onstage, present this award at a time least expected.

5. Be creative and make sure you (or someone you trust) carefully checks each award for spelling and content before presenting and honoring the person.

Don't promise that every award will be handed out. The real lesson is in understanding that it takes a village to excel and remembering to say "thank you." This is more an activity to learn to express appreciation.

This is a fun, crafty exercise that gets the small groups involved – AND could possibly save you time and energy. Have the student groups figure out a fun caption.

Variations

Aluminum Foil Sculptures: This IceBreaker is mentioned in *Ice Breakers 1.* Decorate an award or make a foil sculpture of people that help behind the scenes.

Tech Tips

Homemade notes are most appreciated by non-Millennials, whereas electronic messages, videos and memes are more appreciated by today's tech generation. Regardless, everyone appreciates being recognized for his or her hard work, so do your best to understand the recipient's love language and present their award in a way that is meaningful to them.

ADDITIONAL TECH SUPPORT

Using Technology for Personal Connections

60. Technology Scavenger Hunt

Purpose

Scavenger Hunts are great IceBreakers for the beginning of the school year. Students create memories (and keepsake photos) to remember that first day. This game can also be used as an end of the year party game that uses pent up last-day energy!

Directions

1. Divide students into groups of 4-8 people. Each group needs to have one smartphone or digital camera.

2. Text students a list of challenges and things to find. A group will be disqualified if not all the members are in each and every photo.

3. Give prizes for the most creative photo. Share the pictures with all the students involved.

4. The group returning in record time with all the photos is declared the winning group.

   Technology Scavenger Hunt Ideas

   - License tag with even numbers
   - School newspaper
   - School T-shirt or mascot stuffed animal
   - Build the largest human pyramid
   - Check out a book in the library (extra credit for a pic with the librarian)
   - Folder of music with pencil marking in the music
   - Largest school logo/mascot
   - Spell out the school name with bodies
   - Pick up trash and put in a trash can

Variations

Location Hunt: Create a scavenger hunt to help students learn a new building or campus. Send them to different regions and have them complete tasks related to the activities or services offered.

Tech Tips

One of our favorite apps for scavenger hunts is at Goosechase.com. It offers free classroom "chases" for teachers. Using the app allows you to score points, view results in real-time, and share photos directly to social sites without having to give out your phone number! Goosechase also has a huge number of pre-defined "missions" for those of us who don't have time to invent 50 challenges.

61. Selfie Surprise

Purpose

This game is so much fun, and students will build relationships and cultivate an engaged classroom environment. Use the fun photos to build your social marketing presence. Inside jokes and permanent memories are guaranteed!

Directions

1. Players form a tight circle, sitting on the ground.

2. Open a phone or tablet to the camera app and set it to snap photos with a timer.

3. Start the timer and pass the camera to the right as quickly as possible. As the camera passes, each player needs to keep his or her face in the photo.

4. When the timer counts down, whoever has it in the last few seconds, needs to take the silliest selfie they can!

5. After you take your selfie, you slide out of the circle. Last person to take their selfie wins!

Variations

Quick Picks: Use multiple phones and spread them throughout the circle for a speed round. Instead of stretching it out over a long period of time, pictures will come fast and you won't need to eliminate players as you go! This variation isn't about winning, just about getting silly photos!

Tech Tips

We suggest using a good phone case or a drop-proof camera … people have a tendency to get clumsy as the timer counts down! If playing the Quick Picks variation, try setting all the timers to different lengths for more surprised selfies!

62. Giga-Where?!?!

Purpose

This photo twist on the classic hide and seek game is terrific to play during breaks in an after-school rehearsal or at a retreat. Students will have fun seeking each other out in a non-competitive environment.

Directions

1. One person with a camera (the hidden byte) will be given two minutes to secretly hide somewhere in your building.

2. After the two minutes are up, the rest of the players (the search engines) try to find the "hidden byte." When they do, snap a selfie with them and hide in the same place.

3. As more and more search engines find the hidden byte, the selfie size will grow into a giant hidden gigabyte!

4. The game is over when all the search engines have found the hidden byte.

Use the two minutes while the hidden byte is hiding for another icebreaker or to learn some music! It will help pass the waiting time and create some noise so nobody can hear where the hidden byte is hiding!

Variations

Digital Seek and Hide: Students could be encouraged to post the selfie to an online group or class discussion board as a clue to the other players. As more players are in the picture, more features of the hiding space will be revealed!

Tech Tips

Make sure to create rules and boundaries for when and where students are allowed to hide. An app like Remind or a group messaging app could be used to send out a message to bring everyone back if the game is taking too long!

63. Marketing to the Masses

Purpose

Combine students' love for your program with their creative tech skills to design a commercial. Creative thinking, communication skills, teamwork and technology skills are all utilized in this fun exercise.

Directions

1. Decide the goal of the marketing videos.

2. Divide class into smaller groups and task each group with writing a script. Share the scripts on your school's digital sharing system so everyone can see and edit.

3. Give specific guidelines (i.e. length of time, promotion goal, keep it family friendly, do not use copyrighted materials or music, who is the audience, etc.)

4. Use an app like "Splice Video Editor" or "iMovie" to edit the videos.

5. Choose the video that best captures your original intent. Optional: once the students share the videos with you, put all submissions into a quiz platform, such as Typeform.com, and have the class choose the winner.

Students will get to know each other as they work together competing for the top prize of getting their commercial chosen to represent the program.

Marketing to the Masses Video Concept Ideas

- Promote a new ensemble
- Encourage auditions
- Do a spotlight on student success
- Promote a fundraiser for an upcoming event
- Promote Concert or Event ticket sales

Variations

Music to Your Ears: For the very musical class, you could encourage students to create a song to accompany the video. Free apps like Apple's Music Memos, paired with GarageBand, make it easier than ever to go from a melody to a fully accompanied mp3. Almost every class has at least one songwriter in training that is up to the task!

Tech Tips

Combine shots from multiple phones to create camera angles. Students may need to share video between devices with AirDrop, Dropbox, or a service like Cluster.com.

64. Lip-Sync for Life

Purpose

Engage small groups in a creative team building exercise that builds stage presence and confidence.

Directions

1. Divide participants into groups of 3 to 5 students.

2. Let each group choose a song they all know and love. An instructor could also choose a series of songs they approve of or that relate to course material.

3. Each group selects lead singers and instrumentalists and breaks out to choreograph and practice a lip-sync performance of their song. Give them at least 10 minutes and make sure each group has a device that can play the song for practice.

4. When everyone returns, play the songs over a speaker and have everyone vote for the most outrageous lip-synch performance!

Videotaping the performances is a hoot, and if you have multiple people in the "front row" of the concert video tape, you can splice them all together using any number of video apps available online.

Variations

Weekend Band Warriors: Try giving this out as a weekend assignment. Have groups really put the old college try into the ultimate air band performance. Encourage costumes and props.

Tech Tips

We've already recommended a few quick response tools, like Plickers, Typeform, and Poll Everywhere. Another popular tool that makes creating on-the-fly formative assessment via mobile devices easy is Socrative.com. It is an excellent way to quickly ask large groups questions. Once you've set it up once with your class, the process becomes very fast!

65. Digital Jigsaw

Purpose

Students must communicate and work together to finish a puzzle. Each student needs a mobile device, and the more students you have, the more entertaining this IceBreaker becomes.

Directions

1. Choose a photo of your group or any random object.

2. Crop the photo to a square using desktop software or the edit button in your phone's camera roll.

3. Upload the photo to an image editing app like imagesplitter.net and use the "split" function to divide the photo into the number of participants. Upload the photo to the app. This works best as a grid. If you have an odd number of participants, choose the grid that is closest to you without going over. Example: for a group of 60, a 7x8 grid creates 56 images. Download the .zip of all the images, extract and share them with your group.

4. Now is the tricky part. Each student needs a different image. You can take the time to message them out one by one, or rename the files to student names.

5. Have everyone open the photo and see how long it takes them to create a grid on the floor that completes the puzzle!

This game really works well with large groups of people. The bigger the ensemble, the longer it takes and the more challenging it becomes.

Variations

Instead of using a photo of the group, try using part of a piece of music. You could also use this idea to make announcements about tours, retreat locations, change of venue, or a performance by having students put together a photo of the destination.

Tech Tips

If your students have numbers (such as folder numbers in choir), try using a Bulk Rename Utility to quickly change the names of all the photos to a sequential numerical list. It makes it very easy to tell everyone to go to a shared online folder and download the photo that matches their folder number, and it is much faster than renaming 56 photos one-by-one!

66. Finders, Beepers!

Purpose

Students will need to work together, listen intently, and will learn more about their peers. You will need a secure, large room (i.e. Choir room or stage) or building. This game is played best when you have a whole facility to yourself at an extra rehearsal or retreat.

Directions

1. Choose an area where players will hide their phones.

2. Split your class into groups of 2 to 5 players.

3. Instruct each participant to set an alarm for 15 minutes from now, using the alarm music of his or her choice.

4. Each group is given 1 minute in the "hiding area" to stash their phones while the timers are counting down, safe from prying eyes.

5. Just before the alarms are set to go off, bring everyone into the hiding area.

6. Each participant is to find one phone that is not part of their group by listening for alarms.

7. When all phones are found, make a game out of trying to figure out which phone belongs to which person!

Players need to make sure volume is turned up all the way or the game won't work. For more of a challenge, put phones on vibrate. Students will need to use hyper-listening skills.

Variations

Öi: If you only have one phone, you can do this game with an app titled "Öi - Hide and Seek." The game is simple; you choose a character in the app and lay your phone somewhere. Let your participants into the room and the app randomly makes sounds until someone picks it up!

Tech Tips

Before jumping into this activity, tell your students to make sure they have enabled the locator setting on their phone (such as Find my iPhone for Apple devices) to prevent losing any phones.

67. No Place Like Home

Purpose

This exercise helps you learn a bit more about where students live. Student relationships will strengthen and they will learn more about each other.

Directions

1. Create a secured shared folder where students can upload photos. Some online systems have these built in, or they can always message it to you. Just be clear about what is appropriate to upload.

2. Have students take a photo of some part of their home or dorm room where they spend most of their time.

3. Create a slideshow of the rooms and project them for the class. Make sure to put a sequential number on each slide!

4. On paper, have students write a name next to each number and see who has the most correct!

Variations

If the full room is too intimate for your group, have everyone take a picture of something else that represents them. Ideas include:

- Favorite coffee mug
- Picture of today's breakfast
- Childhood/Toddler photo
- Last book read
- Pet photo
- Phone background
- Car/Mode of transportation
- Most recent birthday present

Tech Tips

Online courses can use this as an IceBreaker as well. Have students take a picture of their computer workstation. If students message you the files, you can post them for all to see and have them vote in a forum! It helps people get to know each other quickly and know a bit more about where they are working. After all, there is no place like home!

Valerie Lippoldt Mack
Wichita, Kansas

Valerie Lippoldt Mack, Chair of Vocal Music and Dance at Butler Community College in El Dorado, Kansas has gained experience and recognition as a music educator and professional choreographer throughout the United States. Her choreography has been featured at Carnegie Hall, Disney World, national ACDA conventions and MENC workshops, the Miss America pageant and various national show choir competitions and festivals around the country. The Butler Headliners were one of four finalists in NBC's *Today's* **"Show Choir Showdown"** and performed for more than 8.5 million viewers. Valerie and her husband, Tom, co-directed the Butler Show Choir Showcase each summer for 25 years. Valerie received a Bachelor of Arts from Bethany College, and a Bachelor of Music Education and Masters of Music Education from Wichita State University.

Her best-selling books, *IceBreakers: 60 Fun Activities to Build a Better Choir, IceBreakers 2* and *Olympic Games for the Music Classroom* from Shawnee Press includes favorite team-building activities and fun games. Valerie's newest resource book, *Putting the SHOW in Choir!* is a great source for teachers, choreographers, administrators and parents. It has been used as a textbook for high schools and college around the county and a top seller since its release in 2012.

At Butler Community College, Valerie directs the Butler Headliners Show Choir, the Smorgaschords Barbershop Quartet, teaches tap dance, choreography and private voice. The Smorgaschords have placed in regional and International Collegiate Barbershop Competitions. Valerie was recently recognized for her outstanding contributions to the Barbershop Society, honored as a Butler Master Teacher, has delivered commencement addresses, and is in demand as a motivational speaker.

In her spare time, Valerie teaches at the Kansas Dance Academy; is active in the Risen Savior Lutheran music program; adjudicates for national show choir competitions, has been on the Music Theatre of Wichita board of directors; and a talent coach for the Miss America program. Valerie and Tom are proud of their children, Stevie, a Commercial Dance major at Pace University in NYC, and Zane, who makes every day a new adventure.

Matthew Udland
Wichita, Kansas

Matthew Udland holds a Bachelor of Music degree from Oklahoma City University in Music Theater and a Master of Music in Choral Conducting from the University of Missouri-Kansas City. At UMKC he conducted and assistant conducted ensembles, worked as a Music Theory assistant, and taught Technology for Music Educators. He has performed across the United States in multiple regional and national tour musical theatre productions. He is an active member and presenter at ACDA and MENC conventions and has been the managing editor of the Missouri Journal of Research in Music Education for seven years. His professional choral experience includes clinician work as well as travel with professional period music ensembles.

At Butler, Mr. Udland conducts the 130-voice Concert Choir, which regularly performs with the Wichita Symphony Orchestra, and Butler A Cappella that performs pop *a cappella* repertoire. He teaches Music Appreciation and voice lessons, and works with the theatre department as music director for musical productions. He has been given the School Bell Award, voted a Student Life Outstanding Instructor, and received the John & Suanne Rouche Excellence Award.

Matthew contracts regularly as a web developer and worked on the team to redesign Butler Community College website. He is an advocate for Purposeful use of technology in the classroom and constantly strives to engage students through meaningful and modern techniques. He believes that technology should serve a classroom Purpose, but is not a substitute for quality preparation and instruction.

In his spare time, Matthew regularly works as a guest clinician and adjudicator for high school festivals and camps throughout the Midwest. He creates toys with small electronics and 3D Printers, is an award-winning pumpkin carver, and loves to travel. He is forever grateful to his wife, Leslie, for putting up with his long hours, her constant support, and head nodding while he rambles about gadgets and gizmos. His greatest creations are easily his daughter, Lucy, and the newest addition to their family, James, born December 2016.

More Musical Resources by
Valerie Lippoldt Mack from Shawnee Press

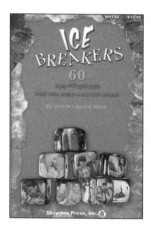

**IceBreakers: 60 Fun Activities
to Build a Better Choir**
(35010427)

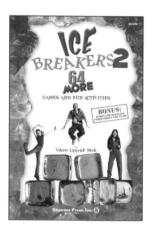

**IceBreakers 2: 64 MORE Games
and Fun Activities**
(35010428)

Olympic Games for the Classroom
(35016005)

Putting the SHOW in CHOIR!
(35027799)

For more information, visit Shawnee Press online at **www.shawneepress.com**

Notes